Purpose, Passion and Profit : Impactful marketing Strategies for Social Enterprises

OrangeBooks Publication

1st Floor, Rajhans Arcade, Mall Road, Kohka, Bhilai, Chhattisgarh 490020

Website:**www.orangebooks.in**

© Copyright, 2024, Author

All rights reserved. No part of this book may be reproduced, stored in a retrieval system, or transmitted, in any form by any means, electronic, mechanical, magnetic, optical, chemical, manual, photocopying, recording or otherwise, without the prior written consent of its writer.

First Edition, 2024
ISBN: 978-93-6554-245-5

PURPOSE PASSION AND PROFIT

IMPACTFUL MARKETING STRATEGIES FOR SOCIAL ENTERPRISES

JACOB JOSE

OrangeBooks Publication
www.orangebooks.in

About Author

Jacob Jose is the Manager of Business Development at PDS Organic Spices in Kerala, India, a pioneering producer and exporter of organic spices, with a mission to develop self-reliant and empowered rural communities in the remote agricultural district of Idukki in the Western Ghats of Kerala. He completed his postgraduate studies in Business Administration (MMH) from Marian College, Kuttikkanam (Autonomous), Kerala, and is currently pursuing a Master's degree in Environmental Science.

In addition to his role at PDS Organic Spices, Jacob has been a board member and coordinator of the Sahyadri Organic Small Farmer's Consortium (SOSFC) since 2016, where he coordinates training and provides technical support to producers. In August 2023, he was elected as the convener of the Indian Fairtrade Coffee Producers Network, where he presented the challenges and prospects of the Indian Fairtrade Coffee sector at the South Asian regional council of the Network of Asia Pacific Producers (NAPP).

Jacob is an alumnus of the ALGOA Organic Foundation Course Master Class, which he completed in July 2022, organized jointly by ALGOA (Asian Local Governments for Organic Agriculture) and IFOAM Asia in Goesan County, Korea. He has actively participated in numerous training programs from various national and international organizations, covering topics such as marketing, organic agriculture, food safety and hygiene, biodiversity conservation, climate-smart agriculture, and the green economy. Jacob is also a member of several sustainability organizations, including FAO's Global Alliance for Climate-Smart Agriculture (GACSA), CII India's National Alliance for Sustainable Agriculture, the Global Forum on Food Security and Nutrition by UNFAO, and IUCN's Commission on Education and Communication (CEC).

Before joining PDS Organic Spices, Jacob worked with the Government of Kerala's Responsible Tourism Initiative, which won the United Nations World Tourism Organization (UNWTO) Ulysses Award for 'Innovation in Public Policy and Governance.'

Jacob Jose

Poovatholil house
Chengalam East P.O
Kottayam district, Kerala, India
Pin- 686585
Mobile: +91 9744268480
Email: jacobpvt@yahoo.com
LinkedIn:

Preface

Welcome to "Purpose, Passion, and Profit: Impactful Marketing Strategies for Social Enterprise." If you are here, it is likely because you believe in the power of business to make a change.

Over the years, I have seen marketing evolve from a tool for selling products to a powerful way to connect with people and drive meaningful change. This book is a result of that belief—that marketing, when done with purpose, can be a transformative force.

Social enterprises are special. They strive to make a profit while also making a positive impact on society. This unique blend brings both incredible opportunities and significant challenges. Marketing in this space isn't just about getting the word out; it is about sharing your mission, building trust, and inspiring action.

In this book, I would like to share, what I have learned about navigating this space. This book is packed with practical advice, real-world examples, and strategies that work. We will cover everything from understanding your audience and telling your story to making the most of digital tools and measuring your impact.

Each chapter is designed to give you actionable insights and inspire you to think differently about how you market your social enterprise. You will also learn about a project that has successfully explored the power of social business to amplify its impact and how to apply these lessons to your own efforts.

My goal is simple: to help you use marketing not just to grow your business but to amplify your mission and make a real difference. Whether you are a marketer or an administrator, I hope this book will be a valuable resource and a source of inspiration.

Thank you for joining me on this journey. Let's create marketing that truly matters.

Jacob Jose

Acknowledgements

I extend my deepest gratitude to all those who have supported and inspired me throughout this journey. To all my colleagues at PDS Organic Spices, your dedication and passion have been a constant source of motivation. I would like to extend my special gratitude to Fr. Jilson James, Executive Director of Peermade Development Society, for his invaluable support and encouragement throughout this endeavour. I also want to thank Dr. Thomas J, Advisor at Peermade Development Society, Mr. Sanu Joseph, Consultant at Peermade Development Society, and Mr. A M Ravindran Nair, COO of PDS Organic Spices, and Mr. Roy Joseph, Deputy Manager- General Administration for their invaluable insights and unwavering support. I am also grateful to my family for their endless encouragement and patience. Lastly, to the numerous social entrepreneurs and change makers I have had the privilege to meet, your work continues to inspire and fuel my commitment to this cause. This book is a testament to your tireless efforts and unwavering dedication to creating a better world.

Contents

About Author .... *v*
Preface .... *vii*
Acknowledgements .... *viii*

Chapter - 1 1
Introduction to Social Enterprises: A Catalyst for Creating Sustainability

Chapter - 2 19
Market Dynamics and Stakeholder Engagement

Chapter - 3 35
Creating Impactful Messages

Chapter - 4 46
Branding Strategies for Social Enterprises

Chapter - 5 50
Explore the Power of Digital Marketing

Chapter - 6 63
Importance of Strategic Alliances for Social Enterprises

Chapter - 7 73
Assessment and Communication of Impact

Chapter - 8 80
Funding and Resource Mobilization

Chapter - 9 85
Scaling the Impact of Social Enterprises

Chapter - 10 90
Importance of Ethical Marketing for Social Enterprises

Chapter - 11 95
  Future Trends in Social Enterprise Marketing

Chapter - 12 102
  Caste Study Vetiver based Women Micro-entrepreneurship:
  Building Resilience through Mutually Benefited Interaction between
  Nature and Local Community

Appendix 112
  Resources for Social Enterprise Marketing

References 118

Chapter - 1
Introduction to Social Enterprises: A Catalyst for Creating Sustainability

At a time when the outcomes of globalization are not as promised, and wealth and opportunities are increasingly concentrated among a small group of people and corporations with profit-oriented actions, social enterprises have emerged as a promising framework that combines profit-making with social and environmental impact. The primary mission of these enterprises is to integrate the triple bottom line—people, planet, and profit—in a more sustainable way to address sustainability challenges that the modern business paradigm has failed to tackle. Alongside profitability, social enterprises aim to prioritize objectives such as employment creation, education, raising awareness, and innovating to address environmental and social issues. To achieve these goals, social enterprises need to adapt their operational and marketing strategies, which are distinct from those of conventional profit-driven businesses. This includes dependency on external funding, collaboration with NGOs, government agencies, and international development agencies, democratic decision-making processes, increased transparency in operations, maintaining stronger rapport with a wide range of stakeholders, and building brand stories that create real-time impacts in the field.

Definitions of Social Enterprise

In general terms, Social enterprises are businesses that operating with a mission to address the challenges of social, economic or environmental sustainability together with their profit making. They are trying to support the local economy through trade and implementing scalable innovative solutions to tackle the environmental challenges. Different countries in the world adopted different contextual definitions for the term "Social enterprise".

The Social Enterprise Alliance of USA defines a "social enterprise" as "Organizations that address a basic unmet need or solve a social or environmental problem through a market-driven approach".[1]

The Social Enterprise Council of Canada (SECC) defines a "social enterprise" as "businesses owned by non-profit organizations, that is directly involved in the production and/or selling of goods and services for the blended purpose of generating income and achieving social, cultural, and/or environmental aims. Social enterprises are one more tool for non-profits to use to meet their mission to contribute to healthy communities.[2]

In South Korea, Article 2 of the social enterprise promotion act of 2006 defines a social enterprise as "an organization which is engaged in business activities of producing and selling goods and services while pursuing a social purpose of enhancing the quality of local residents' life by means of providing social services and creating jobs for the disadvantaged, as an enterprise certified according to the requirements prescribed in Article 7", "the disadvantaged" as "people who have difficulty in purchasing social services necessary to themselves for a market price, the detailed criteria thereof shall be determined by the Presidential Decree", and "social services" as "service in education, health, social welfare, environment and culture and other service proportionate to this, whose area is prescribed by the Presidential Decree".[3]

The European commission describes social enterprises as follows;

A social enterprise is an operator in the social economy whose main objective is to have a social impact rather than make a profit for their owners or shareholders. It operates by providing goods and services for the market in an entrepreneurial and innovative fashion and uses its profits primarily to achieve social objectives. It is managed in an open and responsible manner and, in particular, involve employees, consumers and stakeholders affected by its commercial activities.

The Commission uses the term 'social enterprise' to cover the following types of business:

- Those for which the social or societal objective of the common good is the reason for the commercial activity, often in the form of a high level of social innovation,

---

[1] https://socialenterprise.us/about/social-enterprise
[2] http://secouncil.ca/en/
[3] https://elaw.klri.re.kr/eng_service/lawView.do?hseq=24346&lang=ENG

- Those where profits are mainly reinvested with a view to achieving this social objective,
- And where the method of organisation or ownership system reflects their mission, using democratic or participatory principles or focusing on social justice.

Thus:

- Businesses providing social services and/or goods and services to vulnerable persons (access to housing, health care, assistance for elderly or disabled persons, inclusion of vulnerable groups, child care, access to employment and training, dependency management, etc.); and/or
- Businesses with a method of production of goods or services with a social objective (social and professional integration via access to employment for people disadvantaged in particular by insufficient qualifications or social or professional problems leading to exclusion and marginalisation) but whose activity may be outside the realm of the provision of social goods or services.[4]

The United Kingdom accepts the following definition which is using mostly in the government circles; business with primarily social objectives whose surpluses are principally reinvested for that purpose.

In India, there are no commonly accepted definition for the term Social enterprises. But we can find out some terms like "social ventures" or "priority sectors" used by the government bodies, the meaning of which is very close to that of social enterprise.

Section 2(u) of the Alternative Investment Funds (AIF) Regulations of SEBI defines a "social venture" as follows: Social venture means a trust, society or company or venture capital undertaking or limited liability partnership formed with the purpose of promoting social welfare or solving social problems or providing social benefits and includes, (i) public charitable trusts registered with Charity Commissioner; (ii) societies registered for charitable purposes or for promotion of science, literature, or fine arts; (iii) company registered under Section 8 of the Companies Act, 2013; (iv) micro finance institutions;

Further, under Section 2(v) of the AIF Regulations, a "social venture fund" is defined as follows: social venture fund means an Alternative Investment Fund which invests primarily in securities or units of social ventures and

---

[4] https://eur-lex.europa.eu/LexUriServ/LexUriServ.do?uri=COM:2011:0682:FIN:EN:PDF

which satisfies social performance norms laid down by the fund and whose investors may agree to receive restricted or muted returns.[5]

The RBI has defined the priority sector as including agriculture, MSMEs, education, housing, export credit and others. Categorization of what constitutes micro and small enterprises under priority sector has been made as per the Micro Small and Medium Enterprises Development Act, 2006 ("MSMED") Act[6]

Characteristics of Social Enterprises

- **Purpose:** Social enterprises always have a purpose for its existence which is addressing the local economic environmental or social sustainability. All their strategical decision making are being driven by this purpose.

- **Localised action:** Social enterprises mostly uses resources including human resources from the region they operate. They often consider business as a means to boost the local economy and prevent the economic drain.

- **Collaborations:** Social enterprises are always open to collaborations and building partnerships for fund raising, technical support, networking, marketing and branding. This includes government agencies, international developmental agencies, NGOs and other likeminded organisations.

- **Need based Innovation:** Social enterprises often create innovative solutions to for the issues they are trying to address. They may develop new services, products, or business strategies that address the sustainability issues in their key areas of operations.

- **Transparency and Accountability:** Social enterprises are often go for the business decision making in a more democratic and transparent way. By nature, they are following good governance practices within the organisation and trying to be accountable to their internal and external stakeholders.

- **Social Impact Measurement:** Social enterprises place a strong emphasis on measuring their social and environmental impact. They use a variety of metrics to assess the effectiveness of their activities and make data-driven decisions to improve their impact.

---

[5] https://www.sebi.gov.in/sebi_data/commondocs/AIFregulations2012_p.pdf
[6] https://www.rbi.org.in/CommonPerson/english/Scripts/Notification.aspx?Id=2613

- **Stakeholder Engagement:** Social enterprises actively engage with their stakeholders, including customers, employees, suppliers, and the community. They seek input from these groups to inform their decision-making and ensure that they are meeting the needs of their stakeholders.
- **Profit sharing:** Social enterprises always trying to re-invest their profit into their targeted areas of operations in the form of projects, community support schemes or to their core areas of business itself.
- **Ethical business practices:** Policy decisions and operational strategies of Social enterprises always consider the ethical practices of social economic and environmental sectors such as prevention of de-forestation, payment of minimum wages and other social security benefits to employees, avoidance of hazardous chemicals, reduction of emissions etc.
- **Legal Structure:** Social enterprises can be registered in various forms, including for-profits, non-profits, and hybrid forms. It depends on the geographical area of operation, purpose of operation, type of operation, type of management and distribution of employees etc. In India usually social enterprises are registered as producer companies, trusts, co-operative societies, NGOs, section 8 companies, LLPs etc.

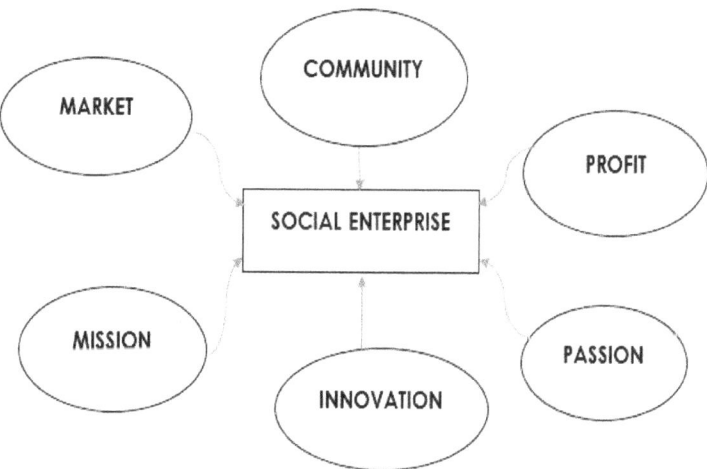

Overall, social enterprises are grass root level organisations having a clear purpose to address the challenges of sustainability. By re-investing the profit in a transparent equitable and innovative way, social enterprises are proving that ethical business practices are the best way for social inclusiveness, empowerment of marginal community and conservation of our planet.

The Role of Social Enterprises in India

Social enterprises play a pivotal role in the India's complex and diverse scenario where the economic and social in equality is below the global average and agriculture still remains the major source of income of the people. The opening-up of Indian economy after the LPG policies of 1990's has widened the disparity between the rich and poor and in the social scenario the gender and caste based in- equality which has been prevailing for centuries, has an accelerated impact in the marginalisation of weaker sections of the community. Access to finance is still a challenge for the poor and marginal farmers and artisans in Indian villages. Also, the environmental concerns like greenhouse gas emissions, pollution, forest degradation, depletion of resources, land use change, overuse of agri-chemicals, waste management etc are burning issues in India. In order to effectively address these sustainability challenges there should be micro-level approach and most of the time our public sector could not able to cater this. The social enterprises have taken on the responsibility of filling this gap with their grass root level organisational capacity, fund raising ability and innovative solutions to meet the challenges. Their approaches are often found to be scalable and adaptable across sectors, allowing them to effectively address the sustainability challenges on a large scale.

In India the social enterprises have been primarily focusing on the following sectors;

- **Financial inclusion:** In the era of paper less currency and digital transactions, one of the challenge the Indian rural population is still facing is lack of access to reliable finance. Financial inclusion is the key driver for, poverty reduction, employment creation, making sustainable living income etc. The committee on financial inclusion chaired by former governor of RBI Dr. C Rangarajan has defined financial inclusion as *"the process of ensuring access to financial services, timely and adequate credit for vulnerable groups such as weaker sections and low-income groups at an affordable cost"*.

  Recent reports show that, in India, since independence, the percentage of the population having their own bank account has increased to 80%. Along with various government policies, social enterprises like micro-credit institutions, small finance banks, cooperative movements, regional rural banks, agri-credit societies, etc. have played a crucial role in this attainment. In order to ensure long-term financial health and inclusivity at the micro level, these supporting institutions should continue their efforts by enhancing financial services and literacy among the vulnerable groups.

- **Sustainable Agriculture:** India's agriculture sector is the source of around 15 percent of the country's GDP and provides livelihood to about half of India's population. Despite this, as per the statistical data of the NSSO, the average monthly income of an Indian farmer is Rs. 10,218, which is a 59% increase from the Rs. 6426.00 recorded in 2013[7]. This level of income is very low compared to other sectors, and the main challenges farmers are facing are price volatility of agricultural produce, an inconsistent market, climate change, exploitation of middlemen, a lack of infrastructure, high input costs, etc. Several interventions have been underway by social enterprises like NGO, start-ups, agri-societies, etc. to meet these challenges with innovation, technology adaptation in farming, the formation of farmer-producer groups, collective approaches and partnership building, credit-linked programs, etc. Organic farming and other sustainable farming methods are often practicing by several groups to address the challenges of agriculture sustainability and increase the revenue of farmers.

- **Value addition of agriculture products and microenterprises promotion:** Several social enterprises are trying to increase the revenue of rural households by developing microenterprises and value addition of agriculture products. Along with income diversification, this approach enables opportunities for employment generation, reducing agriculture-value chains, storage losses, and empowerment of vulnerable groups in rural areas. The major challenges in this domain include lack of infrastructure, technological constraints, access to markets, access to finance, non-availability of skilled manpower, cultural gaps, risk management, etc. Social enterprises are tackling these challenges through collaborations with government institutions, NGOs, and financial institutions, lobbying and advocacy, creating market linkages, deploying trained people, technology adoption, capacity building, training, etc.

- **Rural health and wellness:** Since Independence, one of the primary missions of all the governments in India has been to ensure universal access to affordable and quality health care services for all the citizens, especially in rural areas. India has made tremendous achievements in

---

[7] Situation Assessment of Agricultural Households and Land and Livestock Holding, 2019

this area in the last 75 years, including the number of medical practitioners and infrastructure facilities. But still, there are serious shortfalls in the number of health care professionals and infrastructure facilities in rural India[8]. Also, these systems are not accessible to the rural population due to several reasons including transportation facilities, cultural taboos, a lack of awareness, etc. Malnutrition among children and health issues related to sanitation are still common in rural India. Several social enterprises are working in this field to ensure the mission of universal health care for rural people by building infrastructure, arranging group insurance programs, organizing awareness campaigns and medical camps, etc.

- **Education:** In India education is an area where social enterprises made tremendous impacts since Independence. Several NGOs, trusts and charitable organisations are working in this field with a mission of providing quality and affordable education to the children especially in rural India. Despite of all this, still there is a high level of imparity in the literacy rates in rural and urban India. According to the ministry of education, government of India, the rate of literacy in rural India is 67.77%, while in urban India, it is 84.11%.[9] Major reasons for this gap are lack of awareness, poverty, lack of infrastructure, lack of trained teachers, in-accessibility to schools etc.

- **Technology development in rural areas:** In India where more than two-third of population living in rural areas technology plays a pivotal role in improving the lives and living standards. Several social enterprises are playing in this sector with their innovative solutions in the fields of agriculture, health care improvement, education, financial inclusion, infrastructure development, governance, social development, micro enterprises development etc.

- **Clean Energy:** Another focus area where the government strives to get focused on is clean or renewable energy. Energy security, an increase in the share of clean power like wind, hydro, solar, geothermal, bio, and tidal power, energy access and availability, affordability, and energy equity are the prime missions of government towards this. Several social enterprises are implementing innovative technologies and collaborating with government agencies to achieve this goal of driving India towards a sustainable energy future.

---

[8] Rural health statistics by the Ministry of Health and Family Welfare, Government of India
[9] Lok Sabha Un starred Question NO. 1899 Answered ON 13.03.2023

- **Safe drinking water and sanitation:** Access to safe drinking water and sanitation is a major issue in India, particularly in rural and some urban areas. Contaminated water sources and poor sanitation facilities contribute to serious health problems, such as waterborne infections, which disproportionately impact underprivileged groups. Social entrepreneurs play an important role in tackling these issues by establishing creative, long-term solutions that assure access to clean water and sanitation. Social businesses may close the gap left by traditional techniques by utilizing local resources, encouraging community engagement, and promoting scalable technology, resulting in long-term benefits to public health and general quality of life.

- **Climate change:** Climate change creates substantial concerns for India, such as extreme weather events, rising temperatures, and unpredictable monsoon patterns. These changes endanger agriculture, water supplies, and livelihoods, especially for small and marginal farmers. Social businesses can help mitigate these effects by encouraging sustainable practices and climate-resilient solutions. Social businesses assist communities adapt to changing conditions by introducing new technology, funding renewable energy initiatives, and pushing for sustainable agriculture. Their efforts not only safeguard the environment, but also strengthen the resilience and well-being of vulnerable groups, therefore promoting inclusive and sustainable development.

- **Women empowerment:** Women in India continue to confront various obstacles to reaching empowerment, including inadequate access to education, healthcare, and economic opportunities, as well as traditional standards and gender-based discrimination. Social businesses play an important role in tackling these issues by building inclusive and supportive settings that encourage women's growth and leadership. Social businesses help women become financially independent and confident members of their communities via initiatives including skill development programs, microfinance schemes, and entrepreneurial chances. By overcoming obstacles and supporting gender equality, these enterprises create societal change and contribute to a fairer and sustainable society.

India: Policy landscape for social enterprises

National Level Policies and Programmes relevant for Social Enterprises[10]

POLICY	CONTENT
MSME Development Act 2006, Ministry of MSME	Act establishing legal definitions for MSMEs and providing both a range of national support programmes and a requirement that states do the same.
National Manufacturing Competitiveness Programme, 2008, Ministry of MSME	To build the capacity of manufacturing MSMEs through support and tax preferences. The 'Support for entrepreneurial development of SMEs through Incubators' programme has been operation since April 2008 and is a component of the NMCP (Ministry of MSME, 2014).
Public Procurement Bill 2012, Ministry of Finance	National requirement of 20% procurement from MSMEs, 4% for MSMEs owned by scheduled castes and scheduled tribes.
India Inclusive Innovation Fund 2014, Ministry of Micro, Small and Medium Enterprises	Investment to social solutions with commercial returns (social enterprises) operating at the BOP Domain.
Venture Capital Fund for Scheduled Castes 2015, Ministry of Social Justice and Empowerment	Concessional finance scheme to provide financial support to entrepreneurs from scheduled castes.
Companies Act, 2013 and Companies Amendment Act 2015, Ministry of Corporate Affairs	The Companies Act 2013 came in force in August 2013. It replaced the old Companies Act 1956. The Act focuses the rules, procedures and formalities of incorporating, operating and closure of a company in India.5

---

[10] https://www.britishcouncil.in/sites/default/files/social_enterprise_policy_landscape_in_india_0.pdf

Credit Enhancement Guarantee Scheme for Scheduled Castes 2015, Ministry of Social Justice and Empowerment	Credit guarantee scheme to provide financial support to entrepreneurs from scheduled castes.
Kisan Credit Card Scheme 1998-99, Ministry of Finance, Government of India, Reserve Bank of India and NABARD	Provides affordable and easy-to-access credit to farmers, run by the Reserve Bank of India and National Bank for Agriculture and Rural Development (NABARD).
Enterprise Policy (forthcoming), Ministry of Skills Development and Entrepreneurship	Outlines government approach to support enterprise development, includes small section on social enterprise outlining very briefly what a social enterprise is and detailing planned forms of support.
Alternate Investment Funds Regulation, 2012, SEBI	Regulation which sets out a definition of social venture, for the purposes of social impact investment.
Societies Registration Act 1860, Ministry of Corporate Affairs	Sets out the registration process for on-profit, literary, scientific and charitable societies.
Companies Act, 1956, revised in 2013, Ministry of Corporate Affairs	Sets registration process and legal requirements for enterprise forms.
12th Five Year Plan 2012	With inclusive growth in the title, the plan refers explicitly to focus on innovation.
Samridhi Fund, DFID and SIDBI	A social venture capital fund providing capital specifically to social enterprises India's eight poorest states 6 in specific target sectors7 in order to help scale enterprises which provide economic, social or environmental benefits to the poor.

The Vital Role of Marketing in the Success of Social Enterprises

Social enterprise marketing is the strategic planning and execution of activities by a social enterprise to engage its stakeholders and targeted social groups, fulfilling their needs and wants through the offering of products or services, while also generating profit to re-invest for the organization's purpose. It is a process of creating awareness among customers that their needs and wants are being satisfied, along with their need for altruism. Unlike conventional marketing, this approach not only nurtures a long-term commitment by the customers and stakeholders to the organization's mission but also helps to strengthen their bonds with society. Strategies such as partnership building and stakeholder engagement, impact measurement, and story-building awareness campaigns are crucial elements of social enterprise marketing.

- **Creating Awareness: paving the foundation**

Awareness creation is the fundamental step in a social enterprise's marketing communication so as to educate the customers about the immediate need for partnering with them. Unlike the conventional business who are capturing the market with vibrant advertisement, attractive product and service lines, tempting offers, the social enterprises need to attract and retain customers by creating a feeling of commitment to their mission. According to Simon Sinek's golden circle theory of marketing, successfully communicating the passion behind your purpose is a form of communication with the listener's limbic brain. This is the part of human brain that handles emotions like trust and loyalty, as well as decision-making.[11]

- **Attracting Customers and Supporters: Beyond the Transaction**

Social enterprises always require the support of customers who are not only looking for products or services to satisfy their needs and wants but also want to make an impact on society or the environment through their purchase decisions. The social enterprises can sustain themselves only with the unwavering commitment of their stakeholders, especially the customers, towards the purpose of their existence. Along with the mission, the means of achieving the mission are also part of their unique value

---

[11] https://www.ted.com/talks/simon_sinek_how_great_leaders_inspire_action?language=en&geo=hi

proposition, which attracts conscious customers. It is crucial to formulate an effective marketing strategy that communicates these value propositions and fair and sustainable sourcing, processing, and trading practices to get the support of funding agencies, influencers, government agencies, the media, and NGOs.

- **Building Trust and Credibility: The Keystone of Loyalty**

Building trust with the targeted social group is a vital part of the sustainable growth of any business. For social business, it is more important since partnership building is based on a common mission rather than the transaction of goods and services, which are only a means to achieve it. Only with the synergy of all stakeholders, such as customers, investors, employees, and the general public, can a social enterprise work effectively towards achieving its purpose. Fair and responsible marketing strategies and communications are paramount to creating synergy and achieving the goal. This trust translates into commitment and loyalty, which leads to enduring support from all the stakeholders and increases referrals.

- **Differentiation: Standing Out in the Market**

Along with product innovation, innovative marketing strategies are also crucial for any social business to stand out in a crowded and competitive market. This not only helps in attracting customers who are aligned with their mission but also positions the social enterprise as a front-runner in its area of operations. Reasonable claims, unique brand images, impact stories, unique value propositions, real-time stories, etc. help social enterprises differentiate and position themselves uniquely.

- **Securing Funding and Partnerships: The Lifeblood of Growth**

Securing funds and developing beneficial partnerships are critical for a social enterprise's long-term success. Marketing plays an important role in demonstrating the enterprise's influence, scalability, and potential for long-term success. Impact stories, case studies, and testimonials are effective methods for convincing investors and partners of the enterprise's value and potential. A well-articulated story of impact and success can make funding agencies and potential partners interested in the mission of the social enterprise and open the door for collaborations.

- **A catalyst for Social Change: Advocacy and Influence**

Social enterprises marketing is an effective tool for advocacy and lobbying for driving improvements in the policies related to social and environmental matters. It also acts as a medium of education and awareness creation among the targeted groups in society about sustainable trade practices, fair and equitable use of resources, innovative climate change mitigation strategies, etc. Social enterprises marketing strategies also provide opportunity for partnership building and market collaborations for the unprivileged groups of society which empower their economic and social fabrics.

Marketing thus acts a catalyst for cultivating positive changes in the mind-sets, thinking patterns, perceptions, priorities and purchase decision making process of the customers and other stakeholders.

- **Measuring Impact and Improving Strategies: Data-Driven Decision Making**

Impact stories, reports, and testimonials are the most powerful and effective tools for social enterprise marketing. These not only act as materials for marketing but also as a scale for self-evaluation and progress. By measuring the impacts and tabulating facts and figures, an organization can examine their alignment and commitment to the mission, which opens doors for continued improvements and further innovations. This approach certainly helps the organization boost its accountability and trust with stakeholders.

Insights

For social enterprises, the purpose of marketing is not just about selling products or services but to get mass support for its mission, creating awareness about social and environmental issues and act as a catalyst for societal transformation.

Unique challenges faced by social enterprises in marketing

Marketing is always a challenging role, especially for social enterprises that are working with the dual goal of making profit and creating impact. In all aspects of marketing, such as formulating the marketing content, making branding materials, selecting marketing channels, setting the target audience, allocating funds, recruiting personnel, etc., the social enterprise has to keep in mind these two-fold roles. Comparing with traditional business, social enterprises are facing a unique set of challenges in formulating and implementing these strategies, since along with aesthetic images and well-articulated wording, they have to highlight their values and ethos.

- **Resource constrains**
In countries like India, major challenge a social enterprise faces in marketing is their limited resources such as funds, experienced personnel, and technological support. Unlike large corporates, the social enterprises cannot allocate huge funds for marketing and allocate well experienced staffs for marketing activities. Modern technologies in marketing such as chat boats, augmented reality, AI campaigns, data analytics etc, are often out of their purview.

- **Strategy to Overcome:**
In order to overcome these challenges, the organization can adopt cost-effective channels like social media marketing, e-mail marketing, telephone marketing, etc. The organizations can recruit volunteers, like students' groups or women groups, who are committed to their mission, to do marketing activations and organize promotional and awareness campaigns.

- **Balancing Mission and Market**
Social enterprises should balance their marketing goals with customer expectations. The always upholds its set standards, quality demands, and price expectations. While competing with conventional businesses, whose sole focus is to meet market demand, social enterprises often struggle to do the same without compromising their values and commitments.

- **Strategy to Overcome:**
Creating a unique value proposition without compromising quality and market standards and continuous awareness creation is one way to stay healthy in the competing market. Regular market survey, collection of customer feedback, product adaptation, need based innovation and targeted communication are some other strategy to meet the market demand without compromising the objectives.

- **Differentiation in a Competitive Market**
The market is highly competitive and flooded with information. Differentiating the products or services and standing out in the market is a real challenge for the social enterprises who are operating with limited resources.

Strategy to Overcome:

The linchpin of Social enterprises marketing is their impact story, since story telling is one of the most effective method in marketing communication. A well-articulated impact story with a planned delivery channel will help the organisation to stand out in the competitive market. Community engagement and testimonials of stakeholders and customers also help in this regards. Additionally, endorsements from reputable individuals, government agencies or organisations and ethical trading certifications like Fair trade, Rainforest alliance, B Corp, SA 8000, UTZ etc also support the social enterprises to project its identity to the targeted audience.

- **Communicating Complex Impact**

Just like the value chain and stakeholder profiles, the impact of social enterprises is also very complex and diverse. Especially in a country like India, where there are hundreds of languages, religions, cultures, and customs, it is a monumental task to measure the impact, articulate in a commonly convincing and acceptable style, and communicate effectively. This requires a lot of human expertise, time, money, and other resources.

Strategy to Overcome:

Social enterprises can adopt a participatory style for analysing, compiling and articulating the impact stories with the support of all its stakeholders such as the local community, committed customers, investors, and staffs. They can also use cost effective and online technical resources to make video stories and photo presentations.

- **Building and Maintaining Trust**

When hearing about social enterprises, customers have lot of misconceptions and speculations. Not only with customers, social enterprises have to build and maintain trust with all its stakeholders like funding agencies, local community, staffs, media, government agencies and general public. This process of trust making includes transparency, accountability, loyalty, fairness in operations and commitment to its mission.

Strategy to Overcome:

Certifications and endorsement from government agencies or internationally accepted agencies is the best way to create trust among the public and stake holders. Also keeping a high level of accountability and transparency in the legal and statutory regulations will raise the organisations reputation. Professional customer engagement and responses, consistent communication, social media engagement, ensuring product or services quality etc. are also ways to build and maintain trust for a social enterprise.

- **Engaging Diverse Stakeholders**

Unlike the conventional business whose main focus is solely on customers, the social enterprises have to engage with various stake holders like the local community, funding agencies, government agencies, staffs, customers and NGOs for effective functioning of its operations. It is always challenging to formulate a marketing strategy which is addressing the interests of these diverse groups. The organisations has to take additional care to avoid mutual contradictions and include the contributions of all.

Strategy to Overcome:

A democratic and participatory style of strategy formulation including all these stakeholders can be the best method to tackle with this challenge.

- **Navigating Ethical Marketing**

Social enterprises have to follow their values, fairness, and accountability in marketing communication as well. Unlike conventional businesses that follow aggressive marketing strategies, social enterprises have to respect the ethical standards of marketing, such as regulatory compliance, privacy policies, cultural sensitivity, fairness, and truthfulness, when formulating their strategies.

Strategy to Overcome:

Social organisations need to create and follow an ethical code for their marketing operations. This includes being truthful in advertising, preserving customer privacy, and avoiding deceptive practices. Emphasizing ideals like transparency, justice, and social responsibility in marketing messages can help to promote the company's ethical attitude. Open and courteous communication with customers and stakeholders can increase credibility and confidence.

Insights

Social enterprises operate at the crossroads of business and social impact, posing particular marketing difficulties that necessitate inventive and strategic approaches. Understanding and addressing these obstacles allows social enterprises to effectively explain their mission, attract and retain supporters, and expand their influence. When done intelligently and ethically, marketing can be a strong weapon for social businesses, allowing them to succeed in a competitive market while also driving significant change.

As social companies continue to expand and adapt, overcoming these marketing issues will be critical to their long-term success and contribution to a better society.

Chapter - 2
Market Dynamics and Stakeholder Engagement

Effective marketing begins with a deep understanding of the target audience and stakeholders. For social enterprises, which balance profit with social impact, this task is particularly nuanced. Identifying and engaging the right audience and stakeholders is crucial for achieving both financial sustainability and social goals. This article explores the process and strategies for identifying target audiences and stakeholders for the marketing of social enterprises.

Target Audience

The target audience for a social enterprise is an individual or group of people who wish to make a positive impact in the society or environment by choosing the products or services that satisfy their needs and wants. In order to find out and target these group the social enterprises need to understand the demographics, psychographics, behavioural characteristics, needs and pain points.

- **Demographics**

Demographics is the statistical data about the population in an area and particular groups within it. Social enterprises need to have a detailed analysis of the database of age, gender, income level, education, occupation, and geographic location. By this analysis the social marketing can formulate customer made strategies that targeting the interests and traits of each groups.

Example:
A social enterprise selling organic food products may target urban, middle-income and high income people aged 40 above who are health conscious and level of awareness about safe food, and have money to spend on these foods.

- **Psychographics**

Psychographics, also known as market research or statistics, classify population groups according to psychological variables such as attitudes, values, interests, and lifestyles. A profound understanding of this is crucial for social enterprises because they are mission-driven and need a target group that values the same mission. A database of these psychological characters' helps social enterprises create more personalized and effective marketing communications.

Example:
For the same organic product enterprise, psychographic insights might reveal that they need to focus on customers who value sustainability, have solidarity with farmers, are aware of climate change, prefer natural and organic products, and are active on social media platforms that focus on healthy and eco-living.

- **Behavioural Characteristics**

Behaviour characteristics refer to the customer's interaction with the product or service. This examines the decision-making process of customers, buying behavior, usage rate, expected benefits, brand loyalty, etc. of the target group. This kind of analysis and segmentation helps the business make marketing communication more personalized and increase customer retention. This also supports cost reduction and improved customer satisfaction.

Example:
The organic product enterprise might discover that their target audience tends to research extensively before making a purchase, is influenced by farmer testimonials, and prefers brands that offer transparency about their certification status.

- **Needs and Pain Points**

Identification of the needs and pain points of the target group is critical to positioning the product. Before designing the product or service, a social enterprise must think about the functional, emotional, and social needs of the target group, as well as the pain points such as financial, functional, quality, productivity, support, etc. Understanding these factors enables social enterprises to adjust their products, services, and communications to better meet the expectations and solve the problems of their target audience.

Example:

The target audience for the organic product enterprise may be looking for ways to reduce their footprint, avoid chemical pollution, and support farmer community. The brand can highlight how its products encounter these needs and offer a better alternative to conventional products.

Engaging Stakeholders

Along with the customer groups, social enterprises need to engage with a broad spectrum of stakeholders, which includes the local community, employees, investors, funding agencies, policy makers and government bodies, and media.

- **Customers**

The principal power source for a social enterprise is its committed customers. Customers are the primary stakeholders in any social enterprise. Their support and purchases provide profit for the social enterprises to reinvest in their mission. Along with attracting new buyers, social enterprises also have to formulate strategies for retaining existing customers by providing excellent after-sales services, regular feedback collection, and continuous marketing communications.

Strategies:
- Customer Surveys and Feedback: Through regular market surveys and collecting customer's feedback the social enterprises can understand the needs and pain points of the potential customers, level of satisfaction of existing customers and areas of improvements.
- Loyalty Programs: Loyalty programs such as incentives, discounts, points, etc. not only reward customers for their repeat purchases but also act as a tool for assessing customer behaviour and collecting customer data.
- Personalized Communication: custom made messages and deals based on customer preferences and behaviours is another good way for customer engagement.

- **Employees**

A social enterprise's success depends on its employees. They often serve as front-line ambassadors for the mission, the organisation stands for. Employee engagement involves creating a favourable work environment, giving growth opportunities, and matching their jobs with the enterprise's values.

Strategies:
- Internal Communications: Clear articulation and effective communication of the organisations vision, mission and objectives keep the employees in right track. Also, : Regular communication of the impacts of social enterprises in society and the environment can make employees feel proud and find meaning in their efforts.
- Training and Development: regular trainings and development activities motivates the employees and enables them to enhance knowledge and skills required to perform their job roles.
- Employee loyalty programs, such as rewards and incentives, health and wellness programs, flexible working arrangements, employee engagement activities, allocation of resources, etc., help the organization in terms of employee retention, increased productivity, improved morale, employee satisfaction, etc.

- **Suppliers and Partners**

Building a long term relationship with the suppliers and other partners of the social enterprises is very important for building a strong and sustainable supply chain. Creating venue for mutually benefitted transactions and ensuing fair and transparent dealings are key principles for the social enterprises for a better engagement of this group of stakeholders.

Strategies:
- Transparency: Clear and honest communication about expectations, goals, and performance indicators fosters trust.
- Collaborative activities: Partnering on projects or activities that advance the social mission can improve relationships.
- Fair Practices: Ensuring ethical sourcing and fair trade practices helps to retain integrity and purpose alignment.

- **Investors and Funders**

Investors and funders provide financial support for the operations of the social enterprises. Investors and funders provide the necessary capital for growth and development. Demonstrating the social enterprise's impacts, operational transparency, commitment to the mission, financial compliance, and scalability are the major factors in engaging with these groups.

Strategies:
- ➤ Impact Reports: Regularly publishing detailed reports on social and environmental impact improves trust and transparency.
- ➤ Investor updates: Keeping investors informed about financial performance, milestones, and strategic initiatives builds trust.
- ➤ Storytelling: Highlighting success stories and real – time personal narratives can emotionally connect investors while also demonstrating real-world effect.

- **Local community**

The local community is often the primary beneficiaries of the mission - driven activities of the social enterprises. Engaging community members involves relationship building, addressing local needs, and creating localised action plans to address it.

Strategies:
- ➤ Community Engagement activities: By hosting or participating in local events and activities the social enterprises can foster goodwill and visibility.
- ➤ Partnerships with Local Organizations: Social enterprises can collaborate with local groups or community organisations to strengthen impact.
- ➤ Volunteer Programs: By organising volunteer programmes with the local community for the development of vulnerable communities is another way of engaging with them.

- **Regulatory Bodies and Policymakers**

Regulatory bodies and policymakers have an impact on social entrepreneurs' operational environments. Engaging these stakeholders entails advocacy, compliance, and collaboration in order to foster a conducive ecosystem for social entrepreneurship.

Strategies:
- ➤ Advocacy Campaigns: Lobbying for policies that assist social entrepreneurs and address important social or environmental challenges.
- ➤ Compliance: Following regulations and standards helps to preserve trust and avoid legal complications.

- Collaboration: Working with legislators on initiatives that align with the social mission can result in positive consequences.

Insights

A social enterprise's success depends on identifying and engaging the relevant target audience and stakeholders. Understanding their target audience's demographics, psychographics, behaviors, and needs enables social entrepreneurs to develop effective marketing strategies that resonate and drive outcomes. Furthermore, by developing strong relationships with important stakeholders such as customers, employees, suppliers, investors, community members, and regulatory organizations, social enterprises can construct a supportive network that increases their impact and sustainability. As social companies navigate the complexity of balancing profit and purpose, a strategic approach to audience and stakeholder engagement will be critical to achieving their objective and effecting significant change.

Conducting market research for social impact

Market research is the most effective tool to gather market data such as customer behaviour, price expectations, preferred purchase points, market trends, demographic data etc. Market research is especially important for social enterprises because it allows them to integrate their business goals with their social impact objectives. So it is crucial for the social enterprises to conduct market research for, outlining specific considerations and tactics to increase their social impact.

The Importance of Market Research for Social Enterprises

- Market research offers vital information to social enterprises, allowing them to make informed decisions and plan strategically. Here are some vital reasons why market research is important:

- Understanding the Target Audience: Identifying the social groups who are aligned with the mission and values of the organisation.

- Measuring Social Impact: Measuring and evaluating the impact which the social enterprises created in its targeted area of operations and understanding the areas for improvements.

- Market Positioning: Decide how to position the product or services offered by the social enterprises in the competing market for the best performance.

- Informed Decision-Making: Data driven decision making is crucial for the sustainable growth of any organisations.

> Identifying Opportunities and Threats: Market research helps the organisations to identify further growth opportunities and ways to mitigate market risks.

Steps in Conducting Market Research

Market research is a series of carefully organized stages, each of which is critical for systematically collecting data.

- **Define Objectives and Scope**

Defining a clear objective is the fundamental step for conducting an effective market research. The objectives act as a guideline and for the process of market research.

Example Objectives:
> Find out the level of awareness about the mission of the social enterprise and the perception of the targeted group about the organization.

Measure the efficiency of current marketing strategies and the need for adopting new strategies. placement of the products and services offered by the organization that are addressing specific needs.

- **Develop a research plan.**

A well-drafted research plan contains the process and tools that are being used to collect data from the market. It outlines the type of research, research methodologies, data collection tools, and types of samples to be taken.

Methodologies:

Focus Group Discussions: Interactions with a small group of various stakeholders to find out their perceptions and expectations about the products or services.

In-person Interviews: Interviews are the best method to collect in-depth qualitative data. It can be conducted in person, over the phone, mail, via video call, etc.

Case Studies: A case study is the analysis of specific examples of social impacts and extrapolation to understand a broad spectrum of trends.

Surveys: collection of quantitative data from a large group of people using a structured questionnaire. It can be done directly, over the phone, by mail, or using other online channels and social media platforms.

Online Analytics: Use electronic channels and social media to analyze customer preferences, trends, and behaviours.

- **Data Collection**

Data collection is the vital part of market research, since the success and effectiveness of the entire process of market research depends on the correctness and reliability of the collected data.

Type of data:
- ➤ Primary Data: Directly collected information through surveys, observations, focus groups and interviews.
- ➤ Secondary Data: Data collected from sources like expert reports, studies, publications and other analytical data sources.

- **Data Analysis**

The next step in market research is analysis of collected data to get required information. Data analysis can entail statistical approaches for quantitative data, and theme analysis for qualitative data.

Quantitative analysis involves analyzing survey findings and web metrics using software such as SPSS, Excel, or Google Analytics.

- ➤ Recognize patterns, correlations, and trends that provide information about customer behavior and market dynamics.

To do qualitative analysis, transcribe interviews and focus group sessions.

- ➤ Use coding techniques to uncover common themes and attitudes.
- ➤ Examine case studies to determine lessons learned and best practices.

- **Interpret data and Report Findings**

Making sense of the data and converting it into actionable insights are both required when interpreting the findings. The findings should be summarized in a complete report that includes key insights, suggestions, and strategic implications.

Reporting:
- ➤ Involves summarizing study aims, methodologies, and major findings.
- ➤ Make actionable suggestions based on the data analysis.
- ➤ To effectively display data, use visual aids such as charts, graphs, and infographics.

- **Insights to action:**

The final phase in market research process is to apply the research findings to give insights in marketing strategy formulation and business decision making process. This could include improving the value proposition, modifying marketing efforts, producing new products or services, or expanding social impact projects.

Considerations for Social Enterprises in marketing research

Unlike the conventional business the social enterprises face some unique challenges and consideration in the process of market research.

- **Integrating social impact and profitability.**

Social enterprises must conduct market research that covers both social impact and financial sustainability. This necessitates evaluating not only customer happiness and market demand, but also the efficacy of social programs and initiatives.

Strategy:

Incorporate social impact measures into the research design, such as assessing increases in community well-being, environmental sustainability, or economic empowerment.

- **Engaging Diverse Stakeholders.**

Social businesses frequently serve a diverse group of stakeholders, including beneficiaries, customers, investors, and community members. Each group may have unique interests and viewpoints, making it difficult to collect thorough data.

Strategy: Combine qualitative and quantitative methodologies to capture varied perspectives. Engage stakeholders using participatory research approaches to guarantee their perspectives are heard.

- **Ethical considerations.**

While conducting marketing research for social enterprises, it is critical to maintain a high level of ethical standards to uphold the integrity and commitment to the mission.

Strategy: Make sure the informed consent, honour confidentiality policies, avoid deception, maintain fairness, non-discrimination, professional conduct, and follow all legal compliances.

- **Resource Constraints**

Social enterprises often operate with limited resources, such as manpower, financials, technical, etc., which hinders the effective conduct of research to meet the set objectives.

Strategy: By following cost effective online channels like social medias, mail, bulk messaging etc, the organisations can save the resources. Also by making collaborations with academic institutions and development agencies and by using volunteer services the social organisations can conduct the researches in more efficient manner.

Using Market Research for Strategic Marketing

Data-based strategic marketing decisions are backed by efficient market research, which leverages the socio-economic and environmental impacts of social enterprises.

- **Targeted marketing campaigns**

Use market research information to create customized marketing efforts that speak to specific audience segments. Customize communications to emphasize the enterprise's products or services' distinct benefits and societal impact.

- **Product Development**

Align product development with the needs and preferences found through research. Ensure that new products or services address the pain points of the target audience while also contributing to the enterprise's social goal.

- **Brand positioning**

Make the social enterprise a leader in its area by stressing its unique value proposition and social effect. Use market research data to set the company apart from competitors and create a strong, distinctive identity.

- **Stakeholder Engagement.**

Create engagement tactics that reflect the interests and aspirations of various stakeholder groups. Use market research findings to build meaningful encounters and long-term relationships.

- **Impact Measurement**

Continuously assess and report on the enterprise's social effect, using the metrics and methodology outlined in the research. Use this information to demonstrate accountability, get support, and promote continual development.

Insights

Market research is an essential tool for social companies, allowing them to better understand their target audience, quantify their social effect, and make educated strategic decisions. By performing extensive and ethical market research, social enterprises can improve their marketing efforts, achieve their objective, and effect meaningful change. Since the social business landscape is subject to continuous transformation, the data base of up-to-date market trends and needs is paramount in formulating sustainable marketing strategies to attain the long-term goals of the organization.

Developing personas and understanding the needs

Unlike the conventional business it is imperative for the social enterprises to understand the motivation and challenges of the targeted audience to associate with them in their mission, together with the satisfying their needs and wants. In this process, the personas act as a powerful tool. Personas are fictitious, data-driven representations of a brand's ideal targeted groups. The following are the methods and tactics for creating personas and understanding their needs in order to improve social business marketing efforts.

The Importance of Personas for Social Enterprises

Personas depicts a clear image of the target audience segments, allowing the business to better adapt their marketing messages, products, and services. Personas are very useful for social enterprises since they support to match marketing tactics with both commercial and mission impact goals. Here are some major advantages of crafting personas:

- **Custom-made Presentations:** Craft communications and drives to target precise segments of audience.

- **Product Formulations:** Bespoke products and services that better meet the specific needs and pain points of the target audience.

- **Customer Engagement:** Make stronger connections with your target audience by addressing their individual pain areas and motives.

- **Strategic Planning:** Having a firm grasp of who your target is and what they require can help inform overall marketing tactics and business decisions.

Steps to Create Personas for Social Enterprises

Developing effective personalities requires a combination of study, data analysis, and creativity. The following steps outline the procedure:

Conduct audience research

Thorough audience research serves as the foundation for persona building. This entails acquiring qualitative and quantitative information about your existing and prospective clients.

Methods:- Use surveys and questionnaires to collect demographic, psychographic, and behavioural data.

- **Interviews:** Conduct in-depth interviews with a wide range of stakeholders, such as consumers, beneficiaries, staff, and partners.
- **Focus Groups:** Lead group conversations to elicit attitudes, views, and experiences.
- **Analytics:** Examine data from online analytics, social media, and customer relationship management (CRM) platforms.

Key Data Points:

- **Demographics:** Age, gender, income, education, occupation, location.
- **Psychographics:** Values, interests, lifestyle, attitudes, concern over social issues.
- **Behavioural:** Purchasing habits, product usage, brand loyalty, preference over online-offline.
- **Needs and Pain Points:** Specific challenges they face, issues they seek solutions for.

Group the identified audience

After collecting the required data, the next step is to group the target audience into distinct clusters based on common features. This segmentation will help the business to create more efficient and customised personas tailored for their type of offerings.

Grouping Criteria:

- **Demographic segmentation:** grouping based on age, gender, income level etc.
- **Psychographic segmentation:** grouping people based on their values, interests, and lifestyles.

- **Behavioural segmentation:** grouping based on purchase behaviour, online-offline preferences and product usage.
- **Geographic segmentation:** grouping based on locations.

Example:

For a social enterprise offering organic food products, the organisation might segment the audience into:

> Health conscious adults aged 40-65 who is having income to spent on high cost food.

> Green living: Parents aged 35-45 looking for safe, environmentally friendly products for their children.

> Ethical Shoppers: Shoppers who prefer brands that support farmers and ecology.

- **Create Detailed Persona Profiles**

Detailed profiling needs to be done for each segment based on the distinct characteristics and attributes of each groups. It can be fictional but representative and each persona should have its own identity with name, background story, and detailed characteristics.

Persona Prototype:

- Assign the persona a name and a representative photo to help them become more relatable.
- Demographics include age, gender, income, education level, occupation, and location.
- **Background:** A brief account of their life, employment, and daily routine.
- **Goals and Motivations:** What are they hoping to achieve? What inspires them?
- **Challenges and Pain Points:** What difficulties do they face? What problems need to be solved?
- **Values and Beliefs:** What motivates them? What sustainability issues are significant to them?
- **Behavioural Insights:** How do people engage with products and services? What are their purchase habits?

Example Persona:
- **Name:** Organic Joan
- **Age:** 45
- **Occupation:** Gym Trainer
- **Location:** Urban area
- **Income:** INR 9,00,000 annually

Background: Joan is a gym trainer living in the city. He is passionate about the healthy foods that keep his body and the bodies of his clients fit.

- Goals and Motivations: Joan would like to use and suggest his client foods that keeps the body fit.
- Challenges and Pain Points: He finds it difficult to identify genuine organic food that doesn't contains dangerous pesticides and chemicals that harm human health.
- Values and Beliefs: Transparency, health consciousness and customer satisfaction.
- Behavioural Insights: Joan conducts extensive internet product research, reads reviews, and publishes her discoveries on social media platforms.

- **Validate and Refine Personas**

Personas should be dynamic, evolving as you collect additional data and insights. Validate your personas by comparing them to actual customer feedbacks and behaviours and marketing research data. Refine them on a regular basis to ensure that they are accurate and pertinent.

Validation Techniques: - Gather consumer input to ensure personas correctly reflect their experiences and needs.

- **Sales Data:** Examine sales and customer data to confirm the assumptions made in your personas.
- **Split testing:** Use split testing in marketing initiatives to determine which messages resonate with different segments.

Identifying and Meeting Persona Needs

After designing a persona, the following stage is to identify and address their individual requirements. This entails connecting your marketing strategy, products, and services with the distinct features of each persona.

- **Tailor marketing messages.**

Craft marketing messages that address each persona's specific requirements, motivations, and pain points. Use language and imagery that reflects their values and lifestyle.

Strategies:

> ➤ Personalization: To engage each persona, send individualized emails, run targeted advertising, and create tailored content.

> ➤ Storytelling: Share stories that demonstrate how your social enterprise tackles the unique difficulties and aspirations of each character.

> ➤ Value Proposition: Explain the distinct advantages of your products or services and how they correspond with the persona's values.

- **Formulate relevant products and services.**

Ensure that the offers cater to the individual needs and interests of each persona. This could include creating new goods or changing existing ones based on persona insights.

Strategies:

> ➤ Product Innovation: Use persona feedback and insights to guide product development and innovation.

> ➤ Customization: Provide customisable options so that buyers can adapt things to their interests.

> ➤ Sustainability: Emphasize the offering's environmental and ethical features, particularly for personas who prioritize these values.

- **Enhance the Customer Experience**

Create a smooth and engaging consumer experience that reflects each persona's expectations and habits. This encompasses anything from the user experience on your website to customer service encounters.

Strategies:

> ➤ **User Experience Design:** Make sure your website and digital platforms are easy to use and satisfying for each persona.

> ➤ **Customer Support:** Teach your customer service personnel to recognize and handle the unique demands of various personas.

> ➤ **Loyalty Programs:** Create loyalty programs which honour behaviours that are consistent with your social impact objectives,

such as environmentally responsible purchasing or community engagement.

- **Assess and optimize impact.**

Continuously assess the efficacy of your marketing tactics and the social impact of your business decisions. Use this data to fine-tune your personalities and better your overall strategy.

Strategies:
- ➢ **Impact measures**: Monitor critical measures that show both commercial performance and social effect, such as customer happiness, repeat purchases, and community benefits.
- ➢ **Feedback Loops:** Set up regular feedback loops with your audience to gain insights and make incremental adjustments.
- ➢ **Data Analytics:** Use data analytics to track performance and uncover trends that might help guide future strategy.

Conclusion

Creating personas and understanding their demands is an essential step in developing effective marketing strategies for social companies. By performing extensive research, segmenting your audience, and creating comprehensive personas, you can adjust your marketing efforts to resonate with your target demographic and achieve both financial and social impact. Remember that personas should change as you gain new data and insights. Your social enterprise's potential to generate significant change and achieve long-term success may be improved by constantly improving your personas and aligning your tactics with their requirements.

Chapter - 3
Creating Impactful Messages

Defining the brand story and mission

Since social enterprises are operating with a dual purpose of addressing sustainability challenges, making profit, and targeting a group of audience who are loyal to the same mission as the enterprise, it is vital to articulate fascinating impact stories and communicate them effectively to capture the long-term commitment of the audience. A well-defined mission and real time impact stories are also essential to ensure the unwavering support of all kind of stakeholders from the local community to the funding agencies. This chapter discusses the significance of creating the brand narrative and mission, how to create them successfully, and how they serve as the foundation for the organization's marketing strategies.

The Importance of a Brand Story and Mission

Establishing Trust and Credibility

A well-articulated brand story and mission will help the social enterprises to establish trust and credibility with the target audience. They give transparency about the organisation's purpose, values, and desired impact. When people understand the objectives and relate to the narratives, they are more persuaded to support the business, as consumers, partners, or investors.

Differentiating the Enterprise

In a highly competing market, a distinct brand narrative and mission can differentiate the social enterprise from competitors. By emphasizing what makes the organization unique—like its origin, principles, and the purpose for its existence—they can develop a distinct identity that shines out in their audience's thoughts.

Fostering Emotional Connections

People are always emotionally connected to brands that shares their values and mission effectively. An engaging brand narrative that depicts the purpose of its operations often attracts and retain people who are motivated by the same values. This emotional tie may transform casual supporters into ardent champions for the organisations mission.

Managing the marketing efforts

A well-defined mission and brand story serve as a guide for formulating all of the marketing decisions. They promote consistency in the communication, help the organisation to stay focused on their objectives, and give a framework for assessing the efficacy of their initiatives.

Crafting the Brand Story

Understanding the Purpose of Origin

All social enterprises have its own purpose behind the foundation. This may include the socio-economic and environmental challenges prevailing in their area, a collective dream of transformation, or an individual's efforts and commitment to a cause. This reason or purpose and the actions it is implementing towards the accomplishment of its purpose contribute a substantial portion of the brand story. Before articulating the story, a social enterprise needs to consider the following:

- **Identify the Purpose:** Clearly articulate the purpose of its formation. What motivates the formation of the social enterprise and highlight the significance of this mission and its impact in the society.
- **Highlight the Inspiration:** What inspired the persons or group of persons behind the organisation to take action to address the prevailing challenges. This could be an individual or collective dream about transformation.
- **Illustrate the path:** Articulate the voyage from idea to implementation. Include challenges faced, milestones achieved, and lessons learned along the way.

Defining the Core Values

The core values of a social enterprise are the philosophies that guide its actions and decisions. They define the purpose of the organization's existence and the methodology of its operations. To clearly define the core values:

List Key Principles: Identify and list out the central philosophies that drive the organization. These may contain values such as sustainability, commitment to the local community, innovation, or care for vulnerable groups.

Describe Rationale: Justify how these values and principles are important to accomplishing the mission of the organization.

Demonstrate Commitment: Describe how the organization has been integrating the commitment towards these values and principles in the decision-making process and daily operations.

Communicating the Impact

The brand story also should highlight the impact the organisation aim to achieve. This comprises:

- **Defining the mission:** Clearly articulate the social, environmental, or economic goals the social enterprise standing for.

- **Showcasing Success Stories:** Share real-life stories and case studies that showcases the positive impact the organisation has made.

- **Using Data:** Support the impact narrative with data and figures that quantify the accomplishments and progress.

- Adopting Storytelling Techniques

- To make the brand story appealing, use storytelling techniques that capture attention and resonate with the target audience:

- **Narrative Structure:** Use a clear beginning, middle, and end. Start with the challenges and need for intervention, continue with the actions implemented, and conclude with the impact it made and lessons learned.

- **Authenticity:** Be honest and transparent. Authentic stories build trust and credibility.

- **Emotional Appeal:** Incorporate emotional appeal such as empathy, hope, and inspiration to build a strong emotional connection that motivates the audience.

- **Visual Elements:** Incorporation of visual elements such as photos videos and infographics make the story more capturing and engaging.

Defining the Mission

Crafting a Clear Mission Statement

A mission statement concisely expresses the purpose of the social enterprise and its fundamental objectives. The mission statement should be concise, specific, action oriented and inspiring. It should precisely define the challenges the organisation address, the intended impacts and the approaches adopted towards creating transformation. It should motivate the targeted audience by highlighting the relevance and urgency of the mission.

Aligning mission with the Brand Story

It is crucial to align the mission with the brand story in order to effectively communicate the purpose, values and philosophy of the organisation. Ensure consistency between the two by:

- **Reflecting Core Values:** the brand story should exemplify the core values articulated in the mission.
- **Echoing the Origin Story:** Highlight the key elements of the foundational objectives to generate a comprehensive approach.
- **Supporting the Impact Goals:** Clearly depict the intended impact goals discussed in the brand story.

Communicating the Mission

Effectively communicating the mission of an organisation involves:

- **Internal Communication:** Ensure all team members understand and are aligned with the mission. This nurtures a cohesive organizational culture.
- **External Communication:** Use the mission statement in all the marketing materials, website, and in social media platforms to inform and engage with the targeted audience.
- **Storytelling:** Incorporate mission into storytelling initiatives to highlight the commitment and impact.

Practical Steps to Define the Brand Story and Mission

Conduct Workshops and Brainstorming Sessions

Organize workshops and sessions of brainstorming for the team and stakeholders to encourage cooperation and innovation. Begin by discussing and determining the essential values that define the organisation, ensuring that everyone understands and believes in these ideas. Encourage team members to share their personal stories and experiences linked to the organisation's objectives, resulting in a stronger connection and understanding. Use these findings to create the organisation's brand story and mission statement, then refine them through iterative feedback and conversations. This collaborative approach ensures that the brand story connects honestly with both the team and the target audience.

Follow participatory approach
Contact with the organisation's target audience to obtain useful ideas and comments using a variety of approaches. Conduct surveys and interviews with consumers, partners, and beneficiaries to better understand their perspectives and needs. Organize focus groups to test several versions of the brand's story and mission statement, providing real-time input and conversation. Engage the community in storytelling activities by encouraging people to share their stories and experiences linked to the organisation's impact. This all-inclusive strategy can help the brand to fine-tune its brand narrative, ensuring that it communicates honestly and successfully with its target audience.

Evaluate and Evolve
Constantly review and update the brand's story and mission to reflect changes and development, keeping them novel and relevant. Use the facts and stories from the organisation's impact reports to improve and update the brand story, emphasizing growth and accomplishments. Create feedback loops with the audience to continually collect opinions and recommendations for improvement, establishing a feeling of community and participation. Ensure that the goal and story are still relevant to current social concerns and market trends, displaying the organisation's dedication to solving evolving challenges and adapting with the times.

Insights
A compelling brand story and mission are critical to the success of a social enterprise. These qualities not only distinguish its business, but also foster trust, emotional connections, and direct the marketing efforts. Understanding the significance of a brand story and goal, designing them successfully, and conveying them consistently may help the social enterprise's influence and engagement with their target audience. Embrace these concepts to develop a compelling story that propels the social enterprise ahead, inspiring change and leaving a lasting effect.

Creating a compelling value proposition

The American Marketing Association defines value proposition as the sum total of benefits a customer is promised to receive in return for his or her patronage and the associated payment (or other value transfer)[12]. The value proposition is an assurance by the company's marketing, delivery and after servicing efforts. A compelling value proposition is an essential component of successful social enterprise marketing. It describes the enterprise's distinctive value proposition to consumers, stakeholders, and the society. This session discusses the significance of a good value proposition, how to develop one, and how it can drive a marketing strategy.

processes. A compelling value proposition is an essential component of successful social enterprise marketing. It describes the enterprise's distinctive value proposition to consumers, stakeholders, and the society. This session discusses the significance of a good value proposition, how to develop one, and how it can drive a marketing strategy.

A strong value proposition is crucial for differentiation.
In a competing market, a compelling value proposition differentiates the social enterprise from its competitors. It emphasizes what distinguishes the products or services and why they are important for the intended audience.

Clarity & Focus
A strong value proposition helps the targeted audience comprehend what the organisation is offering and why it matters to them. It directs the marketing efforts, ensuring that all messages and actions are consistent with the organisation's core value proposition.

Customer Engagement
A strong value proposition resonates with the target audience, encouraging them to engage with the brand. At the same time, it addresses their needs and wants, and creating a strong emotional connection.

Impact Communication
For social enterprises, the value proposition goes beyond financial benefits. It communicates the social or environmental impact of its products or services, attracting customers who align with the social enterprise's philosophies.

Creating the Value Proposition

To design a convincing value proposition, the organisation must first identify their intended audience. Conduct market research to better

---

[12] American Marketing Association, AMA Dictionary.

understand their wants, preferences, and trouble areas. Use this information to adapt the value proposition to their individual needs and aspirations.

Identifying the unique selling proposition (USP).
The social enterprise's unique selling proposition (USP) is what distinguishes them from competitor. It might be a distinguishing product feature, a superior service offering, or a distinctive brand image. Determine the USP and include it into the value proposition is an important step in formulating the value proposition.

Articulate Benefits, not Features
Instead of just listing characteristics, focus on the benefits the products or services offer. How does a social enterprise's offering address an issue or enhance their clients' lives? These benefits should be clearly communicated in the value offer.

Aligning with the Brand Story and Mission
An organisation's value proposition should align with their brand story and mission. It should reflect the core values and objectives of the social enterprise, supporting their commitment to creating positive change.

Using Clear and Compelling Language
Keep the value proposition concise and easy to understand. Use language that resonates with the audience and conveys the unique value the enterprise offers. Avoid jargon and technical terms that may create confusion and ambiguity among potential customers.

Testing and Iterating
Once the value proposition is being crafted, test it with the target audience to see how well it reflected in their mind. Use feedback to refine and iterate on the value proposition, ensuring that it effectively communicates the organisation's unique value.

Integrating the Value Proposition in Marketing
Incorporating into marketing messages

Incorporate the value proposition into all kind of marketing communications, including the website, social media, and digital and print advertising. Confirm consistency across all channels to emphasize the core value.

Highlighting in Product Formulations
Use the value proposition as a guiding principle in the product or service development, ensuring that new offerings align with the unique value the organisation deliver to customers.

Engaging with the audience
Engage with the audience by using stories and content marketing to emphasize the organisation's value offer. Use customer testimonials and case studies to illustrate the effectiveness of the products or services offered by the organisation.

Assessing impact
Monitor the impact of the value offer on important metrics including customer acquisition, retention, and satisfaction. Use this data to fine-tune the organisation's value proposition and marketing strategy over time.

Insights
A compelling value proposition is critical for social enterprises to successfully express their unique value and increase consumer engagement. Understanding the customer, finding the unique selling point, and aligning with the brand stories and goal can help them build a value proposition that connects with their target audience and propels the marketing plan ahead. Embrace these concepts to differentiate their business, engage their audience, and maximize their social impact.

The Art of Storytelling: Elevating Social Enterprise Marketing

Storytelling is a great marketing technique, particularly for social enterprises operating with a purpose. It goes beyond typical marketing strategies by establishing an emotional connection with the target audience, making the organisation's mission and impact more accessible and engaging. Here's how narrative can improve social enterprise marketing.

Building Emotional Connections: Stories have the ability to inflame emotions and build a personal connection with the listener. Empathy and long term commitment can be raised by sharing honest testimonials about the individuals and communities who are impacted by the social enterprise.

Humanize the Brand: Storytelling helps the organisation to highlight the human aspect of their business. Highlighting the challenges and accomplishments of those involved in the goal humanizes the brand and makes it more relevant for the audience.

Communicating beliefs and Mission: Storytelling allows to successfully express the social enterprise's fundamental values and mission. Narratives that highlight their goals and accomplishments may make their ideals more tangible and create trust and commitment in the audience.

Differentiating from competitors: In a competing market, a fascinating tale will help the enterprises stand out. Unique and memorable stories that emphasize what distinguishes the business can catch the attention of target audience and set the brand apart from competition.

Stories acts as effective motivator for people to take action. By engaging the audience with inspiring stories of transformation and impact, the organisation can encourage them to support its cause, whether via monetary contributions, purchase, or advocacy.

Simplifying complicated Information: Storytelling can help to make complicated things more understandable. By including facts and statistics into the narrative, an organisation can make their message more understandable and compelling.

Creating a Strong Brand Identity: Consistent storytelling aids in the formation of a strong brand identity. By consistently sharing tales that match the enterprise's vision and values, they can develop a unified and identifiable brand story.

Crafting Compelling Stories for Social Enterprises

Begin with a clear vision and message.

Every tale must have a clear vision and message. Before an organisation begin writing their narrative, choose the main point they want to express and the impact they want to make. The story should centre around this fundamental theme.

Humanize the Story Using Personal Narratives

Personal tales are strong storytelling tools. Share the tales of people whose lives have been influenced by the social enterprise's work, whether they are beneficiaries, staff, or community members. Personal tales personalize the organisation's message, making it more relatable and credible.

Emphasize Authenticity, Challenges, and Triumphs.

Authenticity is essential to great storytelling. Share tales about the true challenges and achievements of organisation's journey. Be open about the shortcomings and disappointments; they bring depth and authenticity to the story.

Use evidence and facts to support the story.

While storytelling is about emotions, it is equally critical to support the narratives with statistics and proof. Use data, analytics, and impact indicators to quantify the influence and impart credibility to the story.

Create an Emotional Connection through Visuals and Multimedia

Visuals such as photos, videos, and infographics can enhance the storytelling and create a more immersive experience for the audience. Use multimedia elements to evoke emotions and create a lasting impression.

Engage the Audience with Compelling Narratives

Engage the target audience with compelling narratives that captivate their attention and resonate with their emotions. Use storytelling techniques such as vivid imagery, suspense, and relatable characters to keep the audience engaged from start to finish.

Incorporating Storytelling into the Marketing Strategy

Align story with the brand identity and mission.

Make sure that the story line is consistent with the brand identity and mission. The story should represent the social enterprise's basic principles and philosophies, emphasizing their commitment for making a transformative impact in the society.

Use Storytelling Across Different Marketing Channels.

Incorporate stories across the marketing strategies, including in the website, social media, email campaigns, and promotional materials. Use consistent messaging and storytelling approaches to establish a cohesive brand image.

Engage the Audience with Interactive Storytelling.

Engage the audience via interactive storytelling events that allow them to take part in the organisation's tale. Use quizzes, polls, and interactive elements to make the stories more interesting and memorable.

Measure the impact of the stories.

Monitor important indicators such as engagement, conversion rates, and brand sentiment to determine the effectiveness of the storytelling initiatives. Use this information to improve the storytelling approach and tell more compelling stories in the future.

Insights

Storytelling is an effective technique for social entrepreneurs to engage with their target audience, communicate their goal, and motivate action. Social businesses can connect their audience on a deeper level, develop trust and credibility, and ultimately drive positive change by writing captivating tales that emphasize their impact, difficulties, and successes. Integrate narrative into their marketing plan to increase their influence and encourage people to join their purpose.

Chapter - 4
Branding Strategies for Social Enterprises

Overview

The American Marketing Association defines a brand as a name, term, design, symbol, or any other feature that identifies one seller's goods or service as distinct from those of other sellers[13]. Like every business, the social enterprise's success and sustainability are heavily influenced by their branding. Branding or brand marketing is the approach used by business to promote and establish a brand in a market by creating a unique identity, values, and insights that differentiate it from competitors. Beyond logos and taglines, it is about changing perceptions, establishing trust, and making genuine connections with stakeholders. This chapter delves into the significance of branding for social enterprise's, its impact on mission-driven organizations, and effective tactics for developing a powerful and meaningful brand.

Define Branding for Social Enterprises

Beyond Visual Identity

Branding is more than simply a logo or visual identity. It incorporates the overall experience and perception of the organisation. It comprises their goal, values, messaging, and the emotional connection they establish with their target audience.

Creating Perceptions

Branding influences how stakeholders view the social enterprise, such as consumers, investors, staffs, and the community. It defines who they are, what they believe in, and why they exist, impacting how people interact with the organisation.

---

[13] American Marketing Association

Building trust and credibility

A good brand establishes confidence and credibility among stakeholders. It conveys consistency, dependability, and authenticity, all of which are necessary to attract and keep consumers, partners, and supporters.

Making Emotional Connections

Branding is about connecting emotionally with the target audience. It's about having people feel something when they connect with the brand, whether it's joy, trust, or a feeling of togetherness.

Branding may enhance the impact of social enterprises.

A strong brand may boost the effect of the social enterprise. It can assist them in reaching more people, attracting more resources, and promoting constructive change.

Engaging Stakeholders.

Branding is an effective technique for attracting stakeholders. It may help them connect with consumers, excite staff, and find investors and partners that match their values and goals.

Differentiation in Crowded Markets

In a congested marketplace, branding may help the organisation to stand out. It distinguishes the company from competition and conveys what makes them distinct and valuable.

Supporting mobilization

A powerful brand can galvanize support for the organisation's mission. It has the potential to unite people behind their vision, motivate action, and build a network of champions and ambassadors.

Branding strategies for social impact

Define the Brand Identity.
Begin by outlining the brand identity, which includes the social enterprises mission, beliefs, and philosophies. Clearly explain what distinguishes them and why their audience should care.

Develop Consistent Brand Messaging
Consistency is key to effective branding. The brand messages should be clear and consistent and should reflects the brand identity in order to catch attention of the audience across all touchpoints.

Develop compelling visuals.
Visual components like logos, colours, and images are effective brand-building tools. Create images that match the business identity and allow the brand to stand out in a visually congested environment.

Engage the audience.
Engage the audience via stories, content marketing, and interactive experiences. Make genuine connections that go beyond commercial relations, encouraging loyalty and long term commitment to the mission of the organisation.

Measure and adapt.
Keep track of the results of the branding initiatives and be prepared to adjust. Use feedback and data to improve the branding strategies and to keep it updated and more efficient.

Mission and Values Alignment
Align the brand identity with the social enterprise's mission and values. The brand should reflect the key philosophies and objectives of the organisation, showcasing their commitment to creating positive change in the society.

Consistency Across Channels
Maintain consistency in the brand messaging, visuals, and tone across all channels. This consistency helps reinforce the brand identity and makes it easier for stakeholders to recognize and connect with the brand.

Engaging Visuals and Multimedia
Utilize visuals such as photos, videos, and infographics to enhance the branding techniques. Visuals can help evoke emotions, create a memorable brand experience, and amplify the impact of the branding efforts.

Stakeholder Engagement Strategies

Engage stakeholders in the branding initiatives by collecting input, including them in decision-making processes, and acknowledging their contributions. Make them feel that they are an integral part of the mission of the social enterprise.

Creating Brand Ambassadors

Encourage the ardent supporters of the social enterprise's mission to become brand advocates for the business. Give them the tools and resources they need to advocate for the cause and spread the message.

Creating shared experiences.

Create chances for stakeholders to engage in shared experiences that are consistent with the brand's values. These encounters may assist to build a feeling of community and improve their connection to the organisation's business.

Collaborating with Like-minded Organizations

Partner with other organizations that share the same social impact goals. Collaborative branding efforts can amplify the impact, reach new audiences, and create a greater collective impact.

Engaging Influencers and Thought Leaders

Partner with influencers and thought leaders who align with the brand values and can help amplify the message. Their endorsement can help the organisation reach a wider audience and increase their impact.

Insights

Branding is a powerful tool for social entrepreneurs looking to have a meaningful social impact. Social enterprises may increase their impact, engage their audience, and promote positive changes by establishing a strong brand identity, generating captivating stories, engaging stakeholders, leveraging collaborations, and publishing meaningful case studies. Branding is more than simply logos, colours, and taglines; it's about changing perceptions, establishing trust, and developing long-term relationships with stakeholders. Using branding as a strategic tool enables social businesses to turn their purpose into a movement, attracting support and encouraging good change via consistent message and audience involvement.

Chapter - 5
Explore the Power of Digital Marketing

Overview

In the contemporary digital age, the marketing environment has shifted dramatically, particularly for social enterprises. Social business organisations, which combine the aims of profitability with the purpose of social impact, necessitate an integrated marketing strategy that stresses both economic success and the achievement of positive social change. This chapter investigates the main digital marketing channels—social media, websites, and email marketing—and how social businesses may strategically use these platforms to broaden their reach, connect with their audience, and develop a community dedicated to their cause.

The Influence of Social Media in Business

Social media has transformed business communication by offering dynamic platforms for engagement, branding, and real-time connection. It enables businesses to access a worldwide audience, exchange information rapidly, and build meaningful relationships with their consumers. Through targeted ads, client feedback, and interactive postings, social media allows businesses to customize their messaging and establish committed stakeholder community. Furthermore, analytics technologies provide insights into customer behaviour, allowing organizations to adapt their plans and remain competitive. Along with cost effectiveness, social media acts as a communication tool that helps social enterprises increase brand publicity, consumer engagement, business growth, and eventually the attainment of their ultimate mission.

Understanding the Social Media Landscape

Facebook, Instagram, Twitter, LinkedIn, and YouTube all have distinctive advantages and target different demographics. A thorough grasp of various channels is required for creating custom made marketing techniques.

The organisation must develop a social media strategy that takes use of each platform's particular characteristics. Facebook is perfect for creating communities and connecting with a varied audience via groups, events, and frequent updates, which fosters a sense of connection and loyalty. Instagram excels at visual storytelling through photographs and videos, so it's ideal for demonstrating the effect of the organisation's social engagement activities. Twitter provides real-time involvement and updates, which is excellent for activism, creating awareness, and participating in social conversations. LinkedIn focuses on professional networking and thought leadership, which are essential for B2B interactions and highlighting corporate successes. Meanwhile, YouTube is known for its ability to combine visual storytelling with a large, engaged audience, making it an effective platform for brand visibility and audience interaction via a variety of content forms such as tutorials, vlogs, and commercials. Understanding and exploiting these various traits allows organizations to develop a complete social media strategy that optimizes their marketing efforts and creates meaningful interaction.

Setting clear goals, identifying the target audience, and providing content that resonates are all necessary components of developing a social media strategy. Key parts include setting goals and objectives, such as promoting awareness, generating contributions, or expanding volunteer participation.

> - Audience Segmentation: Determine the target audience's preferences, habits, and motives.
> - Materials and schedule: Create and schedule material in advance to maintain consistency and relevancy.

➤ Engagement Strategies: Use interactive material like surveys, live videos, and Q&A sessions to increase engagement.

Measuring Social Media Success

The organisation can measure the effectiveness of its social media campaigns by measuring important indicators that are consistent with their mission-driven aims and marketing objectives. This involves tracking engagement rates, such as likes, shares, comments, and follower growth, to assess audience participation and outreach. Additionally, tracking website traffic and conversions from social media platforms can demonstrate the efficiency of campaigns in delivering intended outcomes. Social listening solutions may give insights into audience sentiment and brand perception, allowing social enterprises to better analyse the effect of their projects. Metrics such as the amount of collaborations, mentions, and partnerships may also show the enterprise's influence and network expansion. By monitoring these indicators on a regular basis and altering strategy appropriately, social enterprises can formulate strategies to improve their social media presence, strengthen stakeholder engagements, and increase their brand visibility and impact.

Importance of Website

A website serves as the digital hub for the social enterprise, providing a centralized platform for information, engagement, and transactions. It is often the first point of contact for the existing stakeholders, potential supporters and partners.

- **Essential Website Features:**

The website should be created to give a great user experience while successfully expressing your goal and values. Key aspects include a compelling and informative homepage that clearly explains the objective and attracts visitors immediately.

➤ About Us: A thorough part that highlights the organisation's mission, objectives, the story, introduces the leaders, and explains the influence.

➤ Programs and Services: Provide detailed descriptions of the organisations actions to achieve the mission, emphasizing success stories and achievements.

➤ Donate and Volunteer: Clear calls to action for donations and volunteer opportunities, as well as user-friendly transactional interfaces.

> Blog and News: Provide regular updates on the activities, accomplishments, and pertinent industry news to keep the audience informed and interested. This is a key session in the website of a social enterprises for stakeholder engagement.

> Contact Information: Easy access to contact information and social media connections promotes additional involvement.

- **User Experience and Design**

Smart user experience and responsive design is critical for ensuring the website is accessible and usable on all devices. This entails designing simple navigation with clear menus and a logical flow of information, allowing users to easily discover what they need. Mobile optimization is vital for making the website completely functional and visually appealing on smartphones and tablets. Furthermore, optimizing pictures and content to reduce loading times improves user experiences by increasing loading speed. Incorporating accessibility elements will make the website more accessible to persons with impairments, resulting in a smooth and engaging experience for all visitors.

- **Search engine optimization (SEO)**

SEO is critical for increasing organic traffic to your website. Improve your search engine ranks by implementing tactics including keyword research, on-page optimization, and backlink development.

> Keyword search: Determine and target relevant terms that potential supporters may use to locate your social business.

> On-Page Optimization: Make sure your title, meta description, headers, and content are optimized for the target keywords.

> Content Marketing: Create high-quality, meaningful contents that meets the expectations and interests of the target audience.

> Link creations: Create a plan for obtaining backlinks from reliable websites which are sharing common interests, to increase the site's authority and search rankings.

Email Marketing

Email marketing remains one of the most successful ways to develop and nurture connections with the target audience. It enables personalised contact, building a sense of attachment and loyalty among supporters.

- **Creating an Email List**

Building a strong email list is the cornerstone of an effective email marketing campaign. Tactics for expanding the organisation's list include:

- ➤ Website Sign-Up Forms: Include sign-up forms on important sections of the website, with incentives such as special material or updates.
- ➤ Social Media Promotion: Use social media channels to persuade followers to join the email list.
- ➤ Collect email addresses during events, campaigns, webinars, and seminars.

- **Crafting Effective Email Campaigns**

Developing interesting and efficient email marketing for a social enterprise requires many critical components. Begin by using customization strategies like segmentation to customize content to the interests and behaviours of distinct audience segments, establishing a stronger relationship. Create interesting subject lines that pique recipients' interest and inspire them to read the emails, helping them stand out in busy inboxes. Provide catchy material that informs, inspires, and speaks to the audience's interests and needs, confirming the mission and impact of the organisation. Include clear and appealing calls for action that motivate users to take meaningful activities, such as donations, volunteering, or sharing the material, to successfully increase engagement and support for the social enterprise's goals.[14]

- **Automation and Analytics**

Use email marketing tools to automate campaigns and monitor performance. Automation will boost the phase of communication, and analytics gives new insights for continual development.

- ➤ Automation: Create automatic email messages for new subscribers, contribution confirmations, and volunteer follow-ups.
- ➤ Analytics: Review email performance indicators on a regular basis to determine what works and what alternations needed in the plan.

Insights

For social enterprises, digital marketing channels offer unparalleled opportunities to amplify their mission, engage with a global audience, and

---

[14] American Marketing Association (AMA)

drive meaningful change. By leveraging the power of social media, building a compelling website, and executing effective email marketing campaigns, social enterprises can create a cohesive and impactful digital presence. As the digital landscape continues to evolve, staying informed about emerging trends and technologies will be essential for sustaining and growing your social enterprise's impact.

Strategies for engaging and growing the online community

Engaging and growing an online community is essential for social enterprises seeking to amplify their impact and achieve sustainable growth. A thriving online community fosters deeper connections with supporters, enhances brand loyalty, and drives collective action towards social change. This chapter explores effective strategies for building and nurturing an engaged online community that aligns with the social enterprise's mission and goals.

- **Define the Target Audience**

A deep understanding of the target audience is the foundation for building a successful online community. Identify the demographics, interests, values, and behaviours of the ideal supporters.

> ➤ Audience Research: Conduct surveys, interviews, and focus groups to gather insights into your audience's needs and preferences.

> ➤ Persona Development: Create detailed personas representing different segments of the audience to tailor the organisation's engagement strategies effectively.

- **Align with the Mission**

Ensure that the community-building efforts align with the social enterprise's mission and philosophies. Clearly communicate the purpose of the organisation and the impact they aim to achieve.

> ➤ Mission Statement: Craft a compelling mission statement that resonates with the audience and inspires them to join the mission of the enterprise.

> ➤ Value Proposition: Highlight the unique value the social enterprise offers and how community members can contribute to and benefit from the mission.

- **Building the Online Presence**

Choose the Right Platforms: Select the social media platforms that best suit the organisation's target audience and engagement goals. Focus on platforms where the target audience is most active and responsive.

- ➤ Platform Analysis: Evaluate the strengths and demographics of various platforms, including Facebook, Instagram, Twitter, LinkedIn, and YouTube.
- ➤ Cross Platform Strategy: Create a coherent plan that takes advantage of each platform's unique characteristics to reach and engage various audience segments.

- **Create relevant materials.**

Content is the foundation of community participation. Create high-quality, relevant, and valuable content that connects with the target audience and stimulates participation.

- ➤ Content types: To accommodate a wide range of preferences, use a variety of material types such as blog entries, videos, infographics, podcasts, and live streaming.
- ➤ Storytelling: Share interesting tales that demonstrate the effect of the work, spotlight recipients, and recognize community efforts.

- **Encourage Interaction**

Create a feeling of togetherness by encouraging interaction and involvements. Create opportunities for the audience to engage with the content and with each other.

- ➤ Interactive Posts: Use polls, quizzes, and questions to spark conversations and gather feedback.
- ➤ User-Generated Content: Encourage community members to share their stories, experiences, and contributions related to the mission of the organisation.

- **Build relationships.**

Create true relationships with the community members by being accessible, personable, and empathetic.

- ➤ Engagement Tactics: Respond to comments, texts, and mentions swiftly. Recognize and appreciate community efforts.

➤ Personalization: Customize the interactions to match each member's unique interests and preferences, making them feel appreciated and heard.

- **Host events and campaigns.**

Organize online events and campaigns that unite the community and inspire collective action.

➤ Webinars and livestreams: Create webinars, live streaming, and virtual events to give excellent material and encourage real-time participation.

➤ Social Campaigns: Create social media campaigns that match with the organisation's vision and inspire community engagement through challenges, contests, and joint initiatives.

- **Utilize Influencers and Advocates**

➤ Collaborate with influencers and community activists who share the organisation's beliefs and can help their message reach a larger audience.

➤ Influencer Partnerships: Identify and collaborate with influencers who have a large following and reputation in the field.

➤ Advocacy Programs: Develop programs that enable enthusiastic community members to become champions and ambassadors for the social enterprise.

- **Implement growth strategies.**

Use intelligent strategies to broaden the audience and recruit new members to the community.

➤ Material marketing entails creating and distributing excellent material that drives organic traffic and promotes sharing.

➤ Paid advertising: use targeted social media advertisements and search engine marketing to reach a larger audience.

- **Optimize for Search Engine**

Improve brand's online presence by following search engine optimization (SEO) best practices.

➤ Keywords Strategy: Conduct keyword research to determine the terms and phrases the target audience is looking for.

> On-page SEO: To increase search engine rankings, optimize the website and content using relevant keywords.

- **Encourage partnerships.**

Collaborate with other organizations, influencers, and stakeholders who are sharing a common mission, to reach new people and grow the community.

> Strategic Alliances: Partner with like-minded organizations and businesses to co-host events, create joint content, and support each other's initiatives.

> Cross-promotions: engage in cross-promotional activities with partners to leverage each other's audiences and drive mutual growth.

- **Track and Measure Engagement**

Regularly track and analyse key metrics to understand the effectiveness of the organisation's engagement strategies and make data-driven improvements.

> Engagement Metrics: Monitor metrics such as likes, comments, shares, and click-through rates to gauge community interaction.

> Feedback and Surveys: Conduct regular surveys and solicit feedback to understand community needs and preferences.

- **Adapt and Evolve**

Stay agile and responsive to changes in the community's interests, behaviours, and the digital landscape.

> Trend Analysis: Keep up-to-date of industry trends, emerging platforms, and new technologies that can enhance the organisation's community-building efforts.

> Continuous Improvement: Regularly review and refine the strategies based on insights and feedback to ensure continuing significance and engagement.

- **Celebrate milestones and achievements.**

Recognize and appreciate your community members' efforts and successes to install a sense of pride and belonging.

> Acknowledgment: Publicly recognize and celebrate community milestones, success stories, and individual accomplishments.

> Rewards and Recognition: Use reward programs and recognition campaigns to encourage and recognize active engagement.

Measuring the impact of digital marketing initiatives

Measuring the effect of digital marketing activities is critical for social businesses that want to improve their strategy and show the worth of their endeavors. Unlike regular firms, social entrepreneurs must strike a balance between financial performance and social impact. This chapter discusses several methodologies and tools for assessing the performance of digital marketing initiatives, enabling social entrepreneurs make data-driven decisions to expand their reach and impact.

- **Matching KPIs with Goals**

To successfully assess impact, Key Performance Indicators (KPIs) must be defined in accordance with the organisation's goals. Raising awareness, enhancing participation, driving donations, and fostering volunteers are common goals for social enterprises social media marketing.

> Awareness: Metrics that show how well the campaigns convey the organisations message.

> Engagement: Indicates how actively the audience interacts with marketing materials.

> Conversions: Tracking the activities that achieve the social enterprise's goals, such as contributions, sign-ups, and volunteer registrations.

> Social Impact: Develop indicators to measure how the activities are affecting society as a whole.

- **Setting SMART Objectives**

Ensure that, the KPIs are Specific, Measurable, Achievable, Relevant, and Time-bound (SMART). This helps in creating clear benchmarks for success and facilitates accurate measurement.

> Specific: Clearly defined metrics (e.g., increase in website traffic).

> Measurable: Quantifiable indicators (e.g., number of newsletter sign-ups).

> Achievable: Realistic goals based on the resources and capacity.

> Relevant: KPIs that directly relate to the mission and objectives.

> Time-bound: Defined timeframes for achieving the goals.

Tools and Techniques for Measurement

- **Social media analytics**

Analytics capabilities are embedded into social media platforms, allowing the organisation to measure performance and audience interaction.

  - Facebook Insights provides granular analytics on page performance, demographics, and interaction.
  - Instagram Insights displays information about post reach, interaction, and follower growth.
  - Twitter Analytics monitors tweet performance, audience analytics, and total interaction.
  - LinkedIn Analytics tracks interaction, follower growth, and content success in a professional setting.

- **Website Analytics**

Website analytics solutions provide extensive information about visitor behaviour and website performance.

  - Google Analytics monitors a variety of variables, including traffic sources, user activity, and conversion rates.
  - Hotjar: Heat maps and session recordings let the organisation to analyze how users interact with their website.
  - SEMrush provides SEO and content marketing statistics to help increase search engine presence and content performance.

- **Email Marketing Analysis**

Email marketing systems offer metrics for evaluating the efficacy of the email campaigns.

  - Open Rate: The proportion of receivers who open the emails sent.
  - Click-Through Rate (CTR): The proportion of receivers who click on links in the emails.
  - Conversion Rate: The percentage of receivers who do a desired action, such as contributing or signing up.
  - Bounce Rate: The percentage of emails that were not properly delivered.

Measuring Social Impact

- **Quantitative measures**

Quantitative analytics give solid information about the reach and engagement of the digital marketing campaigns.

  - Reach and Impressions: How many people are exposed to the online marketing material.
  - Engagement Rates: Likes, comments, shares, and retweets.
  - Website traffic includes the number of visitors, page views, and session time.
  - Conversion Rates: The number of successful activities, such as donations or volunteer sign-ups.

- **Qualitative Measures**

Qualitative metrics provide insight into the organisation's projects' deeper influence on the audience and community.

  - Surveys and input: Collect input from the audience to better understand their perspectives and experiences.
  - Testimonials and tales: Gather personal stories and testimonials to demonstrate the effect of the work.
  - Sentiment Analysis: Use tools to determine the tone of comments, reviews, and social media mentions.

- **Social Return on Investment (SROI)**

SROI is a tool for assessing and quantifying the impacts created by the operations of a social enterprise or an NGO. It goes beyond financial returns to include social, environmental, and economic outcomes and impacts to measure the sustainability matrix.

  - Input: Resources invested in the initiatives.
  - Output: Immediate results of the activities.
  - Outcome: Long-term changes and benefits resulting from the activities.
  - Impact: The overall contribution of the activities to social change, accounting for what would have happened anyway.

Reporting and Optimization

- **Creating impact reports**

Compile and disseminate impact reports on a regular basis to demonstrate the efficacy of the digital marketing initiatives to stakeholders, supporters, and the general public.

> ➤ Executive summary: Highlight significant accomplishments and insights.

> ➤ Detailed Metrics: Use visual aids such as charts and graphs to present both quantitative and qualitative data.

> ➤ Narrative: Tell the narrative behind the figures using real-life examples and testimonials.

> ➤ Recommendations: Offer actionable insights and suggestions for future efforts.

- **Continuous Improvement**

Capturing data from measurement initiatives is critical for continually refining and enhancing digital marketing tactics to maximize effect. Use A/B testing to experiment with different content, formats, and techniques to see what works best with the audience and produces desired results. Benchmarking allows the organisations to compare the performance to industry standards and previous campaign numbers, providing insight into areas for improvement and growth. Follow an iterative approach by assessing and updating the strategy on a regular basis based on data analytics and stakeholder feedback, ensuring that the actions are in line with changing goals and market conditions. Furthermore, use predictive analytics and audience segmentation to anticipate trends and customize campaigns, increasing engagement and cultivating long-term ties with the community and supporters.

Measuring the effectiveness of digital marketing initiatives is critical for social enterprises to ensure that their tactics are effective, in line with their vision, and making significant social changes. Social enterprises can gain significant insights into their success by setting clear key performance indicators, using suitable technologies, and adapting quantitative and qualitative data analytics. Regular assessments and continual optimization will help these organizations improve their digital marketing operations, engage their audiences more effectively, and eventually achieve greater social impact.

Chapter - 6
Importance of Strategic Alliances for Social Enterprises

Overview

Partnerships are critical pillars in the journey of social enterprises, acting as drivers for their development, impact, and sustainability. These collaborations go beyond conventional alliances, providing vital resources, knowledge, and vast networks that enable social entrepreneurs to efficiently achieve their objectives. By collaborating with a large spectrum of organizations, businesses, and stakeholders, social entrepreneurs can increase their reach and efficacy in addressing urgent social challenges. This chapter delves into the fundamental benefits of partnerships building for social entrepreneurships, focusing on how strategic collaborations encourage creativity, drive systemic change, and create long-term social impact. It digs into the many forms of partnerships, from community-based efforts to corporate collaborations, and provides insights into successful tactics for cultivating and maintaining these critical ties. This chapter seeks to provide social entrepreneurs with the information and resources they need to build transformational collaborations that move their missions forward and impart significant impacts in the society.

The Benefits of Partnerships

- **Resource Sharing**

Resource sharing through partnerships provides significant benefits for social entrepreneurs, allowing them to reap collective resources for greater impact and long-term sustainability. Collaboration with various organizations, NGOs, enterprises, government agencies and stakeholders allows social entrepreneurs to obtain access to a greater range of resources, including financial assistance from foundations, corporations, and government agencies, in the form of grants, contributions, or investment capital. Partnerships also provide access to key human resources, including experience and skills from partner businesses that improve operational capabilities and strategic planning. Sharing technology tools and infrastructure improves productivity and promotes creativity in social organisations.

- **Knowledge Exchange**

Collaborations between social enterprises and their partners enable a strong flow of information and best practices, which is critical for encouraging innovation and improving problem-solving abilities. Organizations can develop a culture of continuous learning by implementing collaborative training programs and seminars that provide team members with new skills and insights to better face complicated challenges. Partnerships with academic institutions and research organizations provide chances for joint research and development, which drives innovation in products, services, and operational strategies. By using these collaborative efforts, social enterprises not only increase their own capabilities but also contribute to a larger spectrum of stakeholders in their mission, resulting in more impactful solutions that solve societal needs and promote sustainable development.

- **Enhanced Credibility and Visibility**

Partnerships with reputable organizations play an important role in increasing a social enterprise's reputation and exposure, gathering more funds and support from stakeholders. Collaborating with well-known companies and organizations increases credibility through brand association, which indicates trust and legitimacy to the community and potential supporters. Also, collaborative activities and events with recognized partners may attract significant media attention and raise public awareness of the social enterprise's goals and impact. These collaborations not only broaden the enterprise's message, but also develop a favourable reputation, establishing it as a leader in its area of operations and motivate stakeholders to support their purpose.

- **Expanded Reach and Impact**

Collaborations helps social entrepreneurs who are looking to expand their reach and impacts by tapping into partner organizations' networks and audiences. Social enterprises may efficiently extend their global footprint by developing strategic alliances, allowing them to penetrate to new regions and markets that would be difficult to reach on their own. Furthermore, collaborating with organizations that are operating with several demographic groups opens a room for the diversification and extension of the supporter base, and allows the organisations to reach out audiences with a variety of interests and preferences. These alliances not only broaden the enterprise's reach, but also increase its impact, allowing it to connect with a greater range of stakeholders and geographies.

- **Risk Mitigation**

Sharing risks and responsibilities through partnerships is a strategic approach that helps social enterprises to improve their resilience and efficiency. Collaboration with partners allows organizations to optimise financial risk by diversifying financing sources and minimizing dependency on a single source. This shared financial risk not only reduces possible financial challenges, but also promotes financial stability and sustainability. Furthermore, sharing operational duties during project execution helps to reduce operational risks by using the experience and resources of several businesses. This collaborative approach guarantees that projects run smoothly, increases problem-solving skills, and improves overall project outcomes. Also, partnerships that share risks and duties help to create a healthier and flexible social enterprise ecosystem, which is better able to overcome problems and achieve long-term success in pursuing effective empowerment activities.

Types of Partnerships

- **Strategic Alliances**

Strategic partnerships are essential for creating long-term, mutually beneficial relationships that are closely aligned with the basic goals and objectives of partner organizations. These alliances generally take the form of joint ventures, in which businesses pool their resources, investments, and risks to achieve common goals. Joint ventures allow partners to use complementary talents and experience, increasing their aggregate ability to innovate and achieve significant results. Consortia are also collections of organizations that work together on large-scale initiatives or advocacy campaigns, pooling their efforts and resources to confront difficult social concerns or promote systemic change. Organizations may magnify their influence, broaden their reach, and achieve long-term, revolutionary effect by building strategic alliances through joint ventures and consortia that correspond with their common purpose.

- **Corporate Partnerships**

Collaboration with corporate companies provides substantial potential for social entrepreneurs to gain vital resources and experience. building mutually beneficial collaborations enables organisations to integrate good business practices with social impact goals. These collaborations frequently include partnerships that assist a corporate's Corporate Social Responsibility (CSR) programs, in which the corporation offers funds, resources, and experience to develop social projects that are in-line with their CSR goals. Such collaborations not only improve the financial viability of social businesses, but also help to achieve larger community development and sustainability goals. Furthermore, cause marketing alliances comprise collaborative initiatives that promote both the social enterprise's goal and the corporate partner's brand, utilizing their combined reach and influence to raise awareness and generate participation on critical social issues. These strategic collaborations boost the effect of social impacts.

- **Non-profit and NGO Partnerships**

Collaboration with other non-profits and non-governmental organizations (NGOs) allows social entrepreneurs to increase collective impact and operational efficiency. These collaborations frequently take the shape of coalitions, in which organizations or NGOs come together to address common concerns, advocate for legislative change, and raise their voices on crucial issues. By pooling resources, skills, and networks, these coalitions can increase their impact and efficacy in tackling difficult social issues. Collaborations focusing on service integration also bring together numerous organizations to provide beneficiaries with full assistance and holistic solutions. Such collaborative initiatives improve service delivery, decrease workload, and optimize the effectiveness of interventions, ensuring that resources are used efficiently to address different needs.

- **Academic and Research Partnerships**

Engaging with academic institutions and research organizations allows social entrepreneurs to foster innovation and promote evidence-based methods in their sectors. These relationships enable collaborative research initiatives that provide new information, creative solutions, and practical insights for tackling challenging social concerns. By using academic partners' knowledge and resources, social enterprises may increase their understanding of crucial challenges and build evidence-based strategies for improving results. Educational partnerships strengthen these relationships by integrating students and professors in social entrepreneurship activities including internships, research initiatives, and service learning projects. These programs not only give students significant hands-on experience, but they also offer new views and creative ideas to the social entrepreneurship sector, developing future leaders devoted to creating good social change.

- **Community Partnerships**

Collaborations with local groups and organizations are critical to increasing grassroots presence and engagements and optimizing impact for social entrepreneurs. Collaborations with Community-Based Organizations (CBOs) allow social enterprises to leverage local expertise, networks, and community-driven initiatives to solve unique challenges and needs at the grassroots level. These relationships allow communities to actively engage in and own initiatives, which promotes long-term growth and resilience. Furthermore, collaboration with local governments enables social enterprises to connect their operations with rural development goals and policies, ensuring that projects successfully contribute to local economic, social, and environmental agendas. Working collaboratively with community groups and local organizations, social enterprises may utilize collective strengths, establish trust, and achieve genuine change that is based on the needs and ambitions of

Building and Sustaining Effective Partnerships

- **Identifying Potential Partners**

Identifying groups with comparable values, purposes, and goals are essential for building effective partnerships for social enterprises. Conducting extensive research is required to understand potential partners' interests, competencies, and track record. Mission alignment is critical, since it ensures that partners are devoted to comparable social issues and ethical ideals, creating synergies and shared values in joint operations. Furthermore, examining potential partners' competencies and resources is critical in establishing how each business can effectively contribute to the relationship. This involves assessing their capabilities, experience, existing networks, and financial resources in order to increase the synergy of collaborative projects. By carefully selecting partners based on similar values and complementary competencies, social entrepreneurs can develop solid collaborations that maximize resources, boost impact, and realize sustained growth.

- **Establishing Clear Objectives**

Defining clear, equally agreeable and mutually beneficial objectives is critical for forming a successful collaboration for social enterprises. The development of common goals that are closely aligned with both businesses' strategic goals and missions is key to the process. Partners can focus their efforts on attaining meaningful outcomes that contribute to their shared vision of social impact by defining common objectives. It is also critical to define specific roles and duties for each participant in the partnership. This promotes responsibility, clarity, and efficient coordination throughout the partnership's life cycle. Clearly outlining who is accountable for what duties, choices, and deliverables helps to avoid ambiguities and creates a healthy working environment. Initial setting clear objectives and responsibilities, helps the enterprises to create a collaborative atmosphere for both sides.

- **Building Trust and Communication**

Fostering open and transparent communication is crucial for building trust and nurturing a successful partnership for social enterprises. Establishing regular meetings provides a platform to discuss progress, share insights, and collectively address challenges and opportunities that rise. These interactions not only keep both parties informed but also demonstrate a commitment to transparency and shared responsibility. Maintaining open and honest communication throughout the partnership helps to build trust by ensuring that concerns are addressed promptly and decisions are made collaboratively. This transparency fosters a supportive environment where mutual respect and understanding can flourish, enabling partners to navigate common challenges and work towards achieving their shared objectives effectively. By prioritizing regular communication and transparency, social enterprises can strengthen their partnerships, enhance collaboration, and ultimately drive greater impact in their communities and beyond.

- **Formalizing the Partnership**

Formal agreements, such as Memorandums of Understanding (MOUs) or contracts, are required to provide clear parameters and ensure the success of collaborations in social enterprise. These legal agreements explain each partner's scope, obligations, and expectations, establishing a structure for collaboration that reduces misunderstandings and fosters responsibility. These agreements enable both parties to successfully focus activities toward common goals by outlining responsibilities, timetables, and resource commitments. Furthermore, including performance criteria in the agreement enables partners to track progress, quantify impact, and assess the effectiveness of their collaborative activities. This systematic approach not only improves transparency and trust, but it also provides a framework for resolving problems and modifying strategy as the relationship evolves.

By formalizing agreements and establishing clear performance goals, social enterprises may strengthen.

- **Evaluation and Scaling**

Regularly reviewing the development and impact of a partnership is critical for social businesses seeking to optimize effectiveness and achieve long-term benefits. Periodic impact evaluations enable partners to carefully evaluate the outcomes and contributions of their collaborative activities. These reviews give important insights into what works well and what needs to be improved and thereby guiding to strategic decisions and improving the partnership's overall performance. Partners can find opportunities to improve strategies and solve challenges, by asking feedback from stakeholders and reviewing it through impact assessments. This continuous improvement approach increases the relationship while also increasing resilience and flexibility, allowing partners to respond effectively to changing conditions and expand successful initiatives. Also, harnessing information from assessments enables social entrepreneurs to enhance their collaborations.

Insights

Partnerships are vital for social entrepreneurs looking to increase their impact and achieve long-term success. By using partner organizations' resources, knowledge, and networks, these businesses can improve their skills, widen their impact, and drive systemic change. Successful relationships are based on rigorous preparation, open communication, and a shared commitment to common goals. Strategic alliances between social entrepreneurs foster a synergistic environment in which collective efforts generate greater social impact and contribute to a more sustainable future.

Strategies for Forming Partnerships for Social Enterprises

Overview

Strategic alliances are essential for social enterprises seeking to increase their impact, improve sustainability, and fulfil their goal. Social enterprises can benefit from shared resources, expertise, and networks by forging partnerships with similar groups, corporations, and institutions. This session explains various ways for creating effective strategic alliances that drive growth and increase the social impact of social businesses.

- **Definition and Types of Strategic Alliances**

Strategic alliances involve formal partnerships between two or more organizations that share resources and capabilities to achieve common mission while maintaining their independence. These associations can take various forms, including:

> Joint Ventures: Two or more organizations create a new entity to undertake a specific project or activity.

> Equity Alliances: One organization acquires equity in another to form a partnership.

> Non-Equity Alliances: Partnerships based on contracts without equity sharing, such as marketing or research collaborations.

- **Alignment of Mission and Values**

A successful alliance is built on shared mission, values, and goals. Potential partners should have the same vision and dedication to similar social objectives. This alignment ensures that activities are coordinated and the alliance's influence is maximized.

- **Complementary Strengths and Capabilities**

Determine which partners' qualities and competencies compliment your own. This might include technological skills, market reach, financial resources, or other strategic assets. Complementary strengths allow partners to address each other's deficiencies, resulting in a more robust and successful partnership.

- **Reputation and Credibility**

The reputation and trustworthiness of prospective partners are critical. Conduct due diligence to ensure that the partner has a good track record, adheres to ethical standards, and is respected in their sector or community. A reliable partner may help the social enterprise's reputation and bring up new prospects.

- **Networking and Influence**

Study the possible partners' network and influence. Partners with wide networks may help the organisation to broaden its reach and promote the social enterprise to new stakeholders, such as investors, consumers, and community leaders. Influential partners may also advocate for the cause of the organisation and rally supporters.

- **Clear and Transparent Communication**

Effective dialogue is critical for developing trust and understanding among partners. Establish clear communication routes and processes to ensure that all parties are aware, engaged, and in agreement. Regular meetings, progress reports, and open communication may all help to keep things transparent and resolve difficulties as soon as possible.

- **Defining Roles and Responsibilities**

To prevent confusion and overlap, clearly outline each partner's tasks and responsibilities. A formal partnership agreement detailing the scope of work, contributions, decision-making procedures, and dispute resolution systems is essential. This transparency promotes responsibility and seamless teamwork.

- **Mutual Benefit and Shared Value**

Mutual advantages and generate value for all participants are the essential part of a successful partnership. Identify and capitalize on each partner's individual abilities to reach mutual goals. Ensure that all parties involved gain real benefits from the relationship, such as improved impact, cost savings, or better skills.

- **Trust and Relationship Development**

Building trust is essential for every strategic collaboration. Make time for relationship-building activities like collaborative workshops, social gatherings, and team-building exercises. Trust encourages teamwork, transparency, and the willingness to share resources and expertise.

- **Flexibility and Adaptability**

Alliances should be adaptive to shifting conditions and new opportunities. Establish procedures for ongoing assessment and adjustment of the relationship to guarantee its relevance and effectiveness. Being open to change and innovation can help strengthen the partnership over time.

- **Utilizing Technology and Digital Tools.**

Use modern communication technologies like video conferencing, instant messaging, and collaborative workspaces to improve communication and cooperation. These solutions may improve connectivity and keep partners aligned and engaged, regardless of geographical boundaries.

- **Data Sharing and Analysis**

Use data exchange and analytics technologies to track and assess the alliance's success. Data-driven insights may help partners make more informed decisions, measure progress, and discover areas for improvement. Transparency in data exchange promotes trust and accountability.

- **Collaborative Project Management Tools.**

Use collaborative project management solutions to improve productivity, track activities, and manage resources. These tools can assist partners in coordinating activities, establishing milestones, and ensuring timely completion of collaborative endeavours. Examples include Trello, Asana, and Microsoft Teams.

Insights

Strategic relationships are critical cornerstones for social enterprises seeking to scale their impact and secure long-term success. Social enterprises can form dynamic collaborations that drive major social change by carefully selecting partners, cultivating strong connections, and using technical technologies. This session provided a thorough road map for starting and growing strategic partnerships, highlighting the necessity of choosing complementary partners, overcoming obstacles with inventive solutions, and applying best practices. Through these strategic alliances, social businesses not only increase their operational capabilities, but they also empower communities and advance key social causes.

Chapter - 7
Assessment and Communication of Impact

Overview

Measuring social impact is critical for social enterprises to assess the effectiveness of their activities, demonstrate accountability to stakeholders, and continuously improve their operations. This chapter discusses why quantifying social impact is important, the challenges that arise throughout this process of assessment, and the best strategies for accurately measuring and communicating impact.

Demonstrating Accountability and Transparency

- **Stakeholder Demand**

Stakeholders, including investors, donors, consumers, and beneficiaries, want social businesses to show the real impact of their operations. Measuring social impact helps to meet these requirements and building confidence and credibility among stakeholders.

- **Transparency and Credibility**

Transparent reporting of social impact data boosts the credibility of social enterprises. It enables stakeholders to evaluate the organization's performance, comprehend the results of its initiatives, and make informed decisions regarding their collaborations.

For Strategic Decision-Making and Continuous Improvement

- **Data based decision-making**

Measuring social impacts provides useful data for strategic decision-making. It helps to identifying areas of strength and weakness, evaluating the efficacy of various initiatives, and allocating resources for optimising the impact.

- **Continuous Improvement.**

Tracking and analysing social impact data over time allows social enterprises to identify patterns, learn from past experiences, and adapt their strategy to get better results. This method of continuous development is critical for accelerating social impact.

Improving effectiveness of actions

- **Program evaluation**

Measuring social impact helps social enterprises to assess the efficacy of their programs and actions. It helps businesses to modify their tactics for better performance by answering critical questions about what works, what doesn't, and why.

- **Resource allocation**

Social impact statistics can also help the social enterprises in their resource allocation decisions. An evaluation and comparison of the effectiveness and viability of different programs or projects allows social enterprises to utilise their resources more efficiently and maximize their impact while working with limited resources.

Attracting funding and investment

- **Evidence of Impact**

Measuring social impact provides tangible evidence of the organization's impact, which is crucial for attracting funding and investment. Investors and donors are more likely to support organizations that can demonstrate the effectiveness of their work.

- **Impact Measurement Standards**

Adopting standardized impact measurement practices, such as those developed by organizations like IRIS (Impact Reporting and Investment Standards), can enhance the credibility of impact data and make it more compelling to funders and investors.

Improving Stakeholder Engagement and Impact Communication

- **Stakeholder Engagement.**

Measuring social impact enables organisations to consult with various stakeholders to better understand their views, needs, and objectives. This method of engagement can nurture relationships with stakeholders and guarantee that the organization's operations are in line with common interests.

- **Communication and Storytelling**

Social impact statistics can be an effective tool for marketing communication and storytelling. By properly conveying their impact, social entrepreneurs can inspire others, create awareness about social challenges, and collect support for their cause. This data based story telling is an integral part of marketing campaigns.

Methods for impact measurement and reporting

This session explores various methods and frameworks for measuring and reporting social impact, highlighting best practices and challenges in impact measurement for social enterprises.

- **Key Principles of Impact Measurement[15]**

It is critical to approach the assessment of social impacts with clarity and accuracy. First, make sure that the scale chosen are properly aligned with the organization's mission, goals, and stakeholder expectations. This guarantees that the impact measured are accurately representing the genuine result of the organization's activities. Also the credibility is critical; utilizing trustworthy and tested procedures for data collection and analysis guarantees that the impact data are authentic and can be use with confidence. Using defined measurements and standards enables meaningful comparisons of impact data across various programs,

---

[15] Impact Management and Measurement Concepts by investment impact index, SA

organizations, and sectors, which provides useful insights into effectiveness and areas for improvements. Finally, maintaining transparency throughout the measuring process is essential. Organizations can develop more trust and credibility with their stakeholders by openly discussing the methodology utilized, data collected, and any limitations in the analysis.

- **Common Methods for Impact Measurement**

Creating a strong framework for quantifying social impact requires several critical components. First and foremost, a theory of change must be developed. This explains the organization's desired goals and the paths to achieving them and these direct impact assessment activities and highlight the critical metrics.

Second, Social Return on Investment (SROI) is an effective way to measure the social, environmental, and economic impacts generated through the activities of an organization.[16] This includes identifying and assessing results, measuring their influence, and estimating the quantum of social value generated against the resources invested. Third, Key Performance indications (KPIs) are explicit, measurable indications of an organization's success toward its goals, which include both quantitative and qualitative measurements linked to social, environmental, and economic impact.

Surveys and interviews can also capture qualitative data on beneficiaries' and stakeholders' experiences, attitudes, and results, offering useful insights into the organization's impact and success. Finally, impact assessments enable organisations a thorough assessment to determine the secondary influence of their actions in the larger society. This combined information offers a comprehensive strategy to analysing and improving the greater social impact of an organization's actions.

- **Challenges and Limitations of Impact Measurement**

The social entrepreneurs must overcome a variety of challenges in order to successfully analyse and improve the process. One key issue is attribution and interconnection. It might be difficult to accurately credit social impact only to a social enterprise's operations since they are often impacted by a various external factors. Measuring a clear and straight

---

[16] The United Nations Development Programme (UNDP)

relationship between actions and outcomes necessitates rigorous methodology and solid data.

Another issue is data collection and quality. Collecting reliable and consistent statistics on social impact can be especially difficult in resource-constrained environments or when dealing with marginalised people. Limited access to technology, variable literacy levels, and accessibility etc. can hamper good data gathering, resulting in incomplete or misleading results.

Complexity and context make quantifying social impact challenging. Social impacts are often highly complicated and context-specific, making it difficult to use conventional measures and frameworks. Each community or target group may have varying impacts from the same kind of intervention, which demands a more complex and adaptive approach for assessment.

Also, cost and resource allocation are important challenges. Impact measurement may be resource-intensive, necessitating committed people, knowledge, and financial resources. Especially small social enterprises, could struggle to allocate adequate resources for an effective impact assessment, which can risk the accuracy and depth of their assessments.

Addressing these problems necessitates novel techniques, stakeholder participation, and a dedication to continual learning and adaptation in the field of social impact assessment.

Best Practices for Impact assessment

- Stakeholder Engagement: Adopt a participatory style by involving stakeholders, such as beneficiaries, donors, and partners, in the impact measurement process to ensure that their perspectives and goals are represented in the process.

- Use of Technology: Use technologies such as data analytics software and digital data gathering tools, to simplify data collection, analysis, and reporting.

- Ongoing learning and improvement: View impact measurement as a continuous process of learning and development, rather than a one-time task. Use impact data to make informed decisions and review strategies.

- Reporting and Communication: Clearly convey impact data and results to stakeholders via reports, presentations, and other means.

Use narrative and visualization strategies to make data more accessible and interesting.

Insights

Impact measurement is an essential tool for social enterprises to evaluate their efficacy, promote continuous development, and communicate their impact to stakeholders. Social enterprises can gain credibility, attract investment, and optimize their social and environmental impact by implementing strong impact measuring methodologies and frameworks.

Integrating Impact Data into Marketing and Fundraising Strategies

In the highly competitive world of social entrepreneurship, effectively conveying impact is critical for attracting consumers, investors, and funders. Impact data is a strong tool for highlighting the tangible results of a social enterprise's work, making it an essential component of marketing and fundraising initiatives.

- **Building Compelling Impact Stories**

The most successful way to tell the impact data story is to weave it into a captivating narrative that highlights the social enterprise's mission, successes, and future aspirations. This story should aim to engage stakeholders by highlighting the core value of the organization's work as well as its positive influence on communities and the environment. By presenting impact statistics in an emotionally engaging manner that clearly highlights the social enterprise's accomplishments, the organization can strengthen connections, develop more trust, and encourage continuous support and cooperation.

- **Tailoring Impact Messaging to Different Audiences**

Understanding audience requirements is critical for personalizing impact message to different groups, highlighting the parts of impacts that are most relevant to them. Organizations may successfully showcase the value of their work in ways that are most important to each segment of audience by tailoring the communication method, such as proving financial returns for investors or social results for contributors. Using impact data strategically in this way helps to effectively communicate the organization's value offer, encouraging better connections and support from a variety of stakeholders.

- **Demonstrating Accountability and Transparency**

Transparency in reporting is essential for building trust and credibility with stakeholders. By clearly communicating the methods used for impact measurement, the processes of data collection, and acknowledging any limitations, organizations can foster an environment of transparency and reliability. This transparency demonstrates accountability, showing stakeholders that the organization is committed to delivering on its mission and using impact data to track progress and make informed decisions. By highlighting these efforts, organizations can strengthen their relationships with stakeholders and reinforce their dedication to achieving meaningful outcomes.

- **Integrating Impact Data into Marketing Materials**

Creating compelling content is essential for effectively communicating impact. Organizations can increase the attractiveness and accessibility of information by adding impact statistics into marketing materials such as websites, brochures, and social media postings. Infographics, testimonials, and case studies are useful tools for visualizing and personalizing data, making it more relatable and captivating. Highlighting particular real-world examples, such as individual success stories or community initiatives, demonstrates the practical impact of the organization's efforts. These anecdotes not only captivate the audience, but also highlight the significant improvements brought about by the organization's work.

- **Cultivating Partnerships and Collaborations**

Partnership building is critical for social enterprises looking for increasing their impact. Social enterprises can boost their credibility and trustworthiness by demonstrate the impact of their operations and thereby attract effective collaborations from credible organisations, NGOs and corporations who are searching for organisations to work for their sustainability goals. Also showcasing the cumulative impact of existing cooperation emphasizes organizational synergies as well as the larger social advantages obtained.

Impact data becomes a significant product, boosting marketing and fundraising performance. Social enterprises can effectively engage stakeholders, attract support, and drive long-term change in the world by creating compelling impact narratives, tailoring messages to different audiences, demonstrating accountability and transparency, incorporating impact data into marketing materials, and leveraging partnerships.

Chapter - 8
Funding and Resource Mobilization

Overview

Funding is an essential component for the survival and sustainable growth of social enterprises. Understanding the financing options which are accessible is critical for social entrepreneurs for increase their impact, and realize their objective. This chapter gives an overview of the various funding options for social entrepreneurs, covering both traditional and modern finance.

- **Traditional Funding Sources**

Grants are the most common source of fund utilized by the social enterprises. Grants are, non-refundable payments provided by governments, foundations, and organizations to support certain projects, activities or causes. They are often a significant source of capital for early-stage social entrepreneurs, offering critical financial assistance without the pressure of repayment. Grants can cover a wide variety of needs, from operating expenditures to program-specific charges, and are often provided based on the resemblance of project's objectives with the funder's mission and goals.

Impact investing is contributing financing to social enterprises with the expectation of both financial returns and measurable social or environmental impact. This sort of investment, which can take the shape of debt, equity, or hybrid instruments, is designed for businesses that want to achieve good impacts in addition to financial performance. Impact investors want to fund organisations that solve societal problems while also making a profit.

Donations are contributions given by people, businesses, or foundations to help social enterprises succeed. These payments are usually part of CSR funds of corporates, tax-deductible and can be one-time or recurring, providing a flexible and often critical source of funding for social entrepreneurs. Donations can be directed toward general running expenditures or specific projects, and they frequently demonstrate the donor's dedication to the social enterprise's objective.

Crowdfunding platforms enable social companies to raise financing from a large number of people, usually via online platforms. This strategy can be reward-based, donation-based, or equity-based, making it a versatile tool for soliciting financial assistance from the community. Crowdfunding campaigns can generate significant publicity and engagement, in addition to funding, by leveraging the power of social networks and digital marketing.

Social bonds are debt instruments issued by social enterprises or governments to raise funds for social or environmental projects. Investors in social bonds receive a financial return, and the proceeds are used to finance initiatives that generate social benefits. These bonds offer a way for investors to support social good while earning a return, thus bridging the gap between traditional investment and philanthropy.

- **Innovative Funding Models**

Pay-for-Success (PFS) financing,[17] including Social Impact Bonds (SIBs), represents innovative approaches to funding social programs based on achieving measurable outcomes. PFS involves private investors funding initiatives, with repayment tied to the successful achievement of predefined social goals. SIBs, a specific type of PFS, see private investors providing upfront capital for these programs. If the programs achieve their predetermined outcomes, investors are reimbursed by the government or other outcome payers.

Additionally, venture philanthropy integrates venture capital strategies with philanthropic goals, offering financial backing alongside strategic guidance and capacity-building support to social enterprises. Impact accelerators and incubators further strengthen these efforts by providing funding, mentorship, and networking opportunities, helping social enterprises to expand their reach and effectiveness through structured programs and pitch events.

Together, these financing models aim to drive social innovation and sustainable impact in diverse communities worldwide. Social venture capital funds invest in social enterprises with the expectation of both financial returns and social impact. These funds typically target early-stage or high-growth social enterprises. Together, these financing models aim to

---

[17] Stanford social innovation review

drive social innovation and sustainable impact in diverse communities worldwide.

- **Challenges and Considerations**

Access to money: Many social enterprises, particularly those in poor nations or rural regions, struggle to obtain money owing to inadequate resources and a lack of knowledge about possible funding sources.

Impact assessment: Investors and funders are increasingly expecting social entrepreneurs to demonstrate their impact, which can be difficult for groups with low capability for efficient impact assessment.

Financial Sustainability: Social enterprises often face the problem of balancing financial sustainability and social impact. Finding the correct balance of financial sources and revenue-generating activities is critical to long-term success.

Regulatory environment: The regulatory environment for social enterprises differs by nation, affecting their capacity to get certain forms of finance or engage in specified activities.

Strategies for fundraising and resource mobilization

Overview

Social enterprises can adopt a variety of strategies to acquire and sustain funds for their sustainable operations. Familiarity with many funding choices and their requirements is critical for social entrepreneurs trying to acquire the resources needed to propel their purpose forward and spark long-term social impact.

- **Diversifying Funding Sources**

Financial assistance through grants, impact investments, contributions, and earned revenue streams is critical for social enterprise's long-term sustainability and growth. Grants are vital financing sources from government agencies, charities, and groups that share the enterprise's mission and aims. Impact investing entails connecting with investors who are interested in attaining both social and environmental impact and financial returns, providing a chance to market the enterprise's unique value proposition. Donations are critical, necessitating a well-planned fundraising approach that targets people, organizations, and foundations interested in giving to social issues. Furthermore, looking into earned income opportunities—such as selling products or services that fit the company's mission—can help to diversify revenue sources and improve financial stability. Together, these funding solutions help social entrepreneurs achieve their goals while negotiating the hurdles of financial sustainability and social impact.

- **Building Relationships with Donors and Investors**

Strong ties with funders and impact investors are critical for the long-term viability of social businesses. Cultivating donor relationships entails a strong stewardship strategy that continuously engages contributors and keeps them informed about the practical impacts of their donations. This method not only promotes trust and loyalty, but it also encourages ongoing support and commitment. Engaging impact investors necessitates proactive networking initiatives, such as participation in relevant events and pitch competitions where the organisation can demonstrate its mission-driven accomplishments and potential for scalable impact. Demonstrating impact through appealing statistics and stories boosts trust with funders and investors by demonstrating the enterprise's efficacy in driving real social change. By concentrating on these practices, social enterprises can effectively acquire and maintain critical financial backing while also promoting their founding mission.

- **Leveraging Technology for Fundraising**

Modern social enterprises must use digital tools and platforms to increase their fundraising reach and effect. Online fundraising platforms, such as crowdfunding websites, enable the organisation to engage a large audience and raise money for specific projects or initiatives, using the power of collective support. Social media platforms are effective venues for sharing interesting stories, interacting directly with supporters, and raising awareness about the organization's goal and successes. Implementing user-friendly contribution interfaces on the enterprise's website and social media platforms improves accessibility, making it easier for donors to contribute and support the cause. These digital techniques not only increase awareness and engagement but also create genuine interactions with supporters.

- **Collaborating with Partners and Stakeholders**

Effective collaboration and stakeholder involvement are critical techniques for increasing the impact and sustainability of social businesses. Collaborations with different entities such as other organizations, corporations, and government agencies allow social entrepreneurs to get access to new financing possibilities, knowledge, and resources, therefore increasing their potential to create real social change.

These collaborations not only increase the reach of projects, but they also promote innovation and scalability. Engaging stakeholders, including beneficiaries, community members, and contributors, is also critical for developing meaningful connections, gaining support, and creating trust in the organization's mission and operations. Social enterprises can create a supporting environment that promotes long-term success and sustainable growth by actively integrating stakeholders in decision-making processes and continuously explaining the positive effects of their participation.

- **Monitoring and evaluation**

Monitoring and evaluation are critical for social enterprises to demonstrate impact and responsibility. Implementing a strong impact assessment system allows the organisation to track program outcomes more effectively, delivering useful insights to funders and investors. Maintaining strong financial management procedures, as well as transparency and accountability in budgeting and financial reporting, is equally important. These initiatives not only foster stakeholder confidence, but also help to ensure long-term sustainability by demonstrating the organization's capacity to carry out its goal effectively and ethically.

Insights

Effective fundraising and resource mobilization are essential for the success and sustainability of social enterprises. By diversifying funding sources, building relationships with donors and investors, leveraging technology, collaborating with partners, and implementing robust monitoring and evaluation systems, social enterprises can secure the resources they need to achieve their mission and create lasting social impact.

Chapter - 9
Scaling the Impact of Social Enterprises

Overview

Scaling a social enterprise requires careful planning, strategic partnerships, robust financial management, organizational capacity building, and a commitment to monitoring, evaluation, and continuous learning. By following these strategies and best practices, social enterprises can effectively scale their impact, reach more beneficiaries, and create lasting social change. This chapter delves into in-depth methods and best practices for growing social businesses while retaining their mission, values, and impact.

Developing a Scalable Model

- Scalability Assessment: Evaluate the organization's scalability, taking into account market demand, operational capacity, and financial feasibility.

- Replicability: Create a model that is easily duplicated or adaptable to multiple contexts or geographies while maintaining the same impact and quality.

- Technology Integration: Use technologies to simplify procedures, increase productivity, and reach a wider audience. Consider using digital platforms, data analytics, and automation solutions to help in scaling operations.

Strategic Partnerships and Collaborations

- Partner Selection: Find and work with key partners, such as investors, donors, governments, and other organizations, to offer funds, knowledge, and resources for scaling.

- Co-Creation: Engage partners in the development of scalable solutions, utilizing their knowledge and networks to increase effect and reach.

- Network Expansion: Build a larger network of supporters, including beneficiaries, community members, and stakeholders, to boost visibility, credibility, and resource availability.

Financial Planning and Resource Mobilization

- Diversified financing: Create a financing plan that incorporates grants, impact investment, contributions, earned income, and other revenue streams to help with growing initiatives.

- Financial Management: Use strong financial management methods to analyze spending, manage cash flow, and provide financial stability during the scaling process.

- Impact Investment: Attract impact investors that share the organisation's vision and aims and can contribute stable financial support to enable long-term sustainability and impact.

Organizational Capacity Building

- Leadership Development: Invest in developing strong leadership and management capabilities to drive scaling efforts and navigate the challenges of growth.

- Talent Acquisition: Recruit and retain top talent with the skills and expertise needed to support scaling, including operations, marketing, finance, and technology.

- Learning Culture: Foster a culture of learning, innovation, and adaptability, where employees are encouraged to experiment, take risks, and learn from failures.

Monitoring, Evaluating, and Learning

- Impact Measurement: Establish clear metrics and indicators to measure the impact of scaling efforts, and use this data to make informed decisions and drive continuous improvement.

- Feedback Mechanisms: Collect feedback from stakeholders, including beneficiaries, partners, and employees, to gather insights, identify challenges, and adapt scaling strategies accordingly.

- Knowledge Sharing: Share lessons learned and best practices with the broader stakeholder community to contribute to collective learning and advancement in the sector.

Challenges and considerations for scaling

- **Financial Sustainability**

Scaling social enterprises presents several obstacles which need strategic planning and careful management. Finding sustainable financial source is one of the major challenge, particularly in the early phases, when restricted access to capital and dependence on limited number of donors can hinder progress. Furthermore, striking a balance between money generation and social impact remains a key problem. Social enterprises must develop sustainable revenue sources while remaining committed to their primary mission and values. Furthermore, growing increases financial complexity, needs strong financial management procedures that include budgeting, cash flow management, and rigorous reporting. Addressing these obstacles effectively is critical for expanding organizations to maintain their impact, attract future investment, and achieve long-term success in promoting social goals.

- **Operational Capacity**

Maintaining operational efficiency, human resources management, and building technological infrastructure are some of the major challenges in scaling social enterprises, which should be carefully addressed and strategically managed. Ensuring operational scalability entails increasing capacity to meet growing demand while maintaining quality and impact, a difficult balance that necessitates efficient resource allocation and process optimization. Human resources are another difficulty, since growing demands hiring and maintaining qualified workers, developing leadership skills, and cultivating a synergetic organizational culture that is consistent with the enterprise's mission. Also, investing in technology and infrastructure is critical for enabling scalability, which includes digital platforms, strong data management systems, and optimized operational procedures. These expenditures are critical for improving efficiency, reaching a larger audience, and sustaining operational quality while growing.

- **Impact Measurement and Evaluation**

Effectively managing and imparting social impact is a critical problem for scaling social enterprises, especially as they grow. Defining and quantifying impact in a meaningful and logical way becomes more difficult as the organization grows. Implementing strong monitoring and evaluation systems are critical for tracking impact, collecting relevant data, and making informed strategic decisions, but it frequently requires substantial money and experience. Furthermore, cultivating a culture of continuous learning, innovation, and adaptation is crucial for expanding businesses to handle proactively to evolving challenges and opportunities. This includes not just introducing a culture of improvement and innovation in employees, but also devoting resources to support continuing training and development efforts.

- **Stakeholder Engagement and Partnerships**

Building and retaining trust with multiple stakeholders is critical for developing social enterprises. Engaging with beneficiaries, donors, investors, and partners to align interests and gain support necessitates consistent effort and open communication. Effective relationship management requires proactive communication, managing needs and expectations, and guaranteeing mutual benefit in partnerships and collaborations. This requires open communication and responsibility in order to establish long-term partnerships based on trust and shared mission. Balancing the different interests of stakeholders—from financial investors seeking profits to social impact investors focused on results and beneficiaries expecting actual benefits—increases complexity. To successfully navigate these dynamics, objectives must be strategically aligned, and ongoing engagements and adaptable solutions should be nurtured. Scaling social enterprises that prioritize trust-building, effective relationship management, and stakeholder alignment can promote long-term relationships and optimize their synergetic effects on society.

- **Regulatory and Policy Environment**

Managing the legal and regulatory landscape, which includes tax regulations, reporting obligations, and licensing requirements, offers substantial challenges that necessitate thorough attention and skill to assure compliance and avoid severe consequences. Advocating for laws and regulations that promote the growth and sustainability of social enterprises is a long-term activity that necessitates coordination with legislators and advocacy organizations in order to positively impact systemic change in the legal structures. Also, adjusting to changing market dynamics, competitive challenges, and variations in consumer behaviour is critical for expanding organisations to remain relevant and capitalize on growth possibilities. To effectively navigate uncertainty and capitalize on new trends, strategic planning must be responsive, along with operational flexibility. By proactively tackling these obstacles, social enterprises can strengthen their operational resilience, create a favourable regulatory environment, and capitalise on market potentials to achieve long-term goals and optimize their societal impact.

Insights

Scaling a social enterprise presents a range of challenges, including financial sustainability, operational capacity, impact measurement, stakeholder engagement, and regulatory compliance. By understanding these challenges and implementing strategies to address them, social enterprises can overcome barriers to scaling and maximize their impact and sustainability.

Jacob Jose

Chapter - 10
Importance of Ethical Marketing for Social Enterprises

Overview

In the world of social entrepreneurship, where the purpose is as important as the product or service, ethical marketing is more than simply an option; it is a need for success. This chapter digs into the complex landscape of ethical marketing for social businesses, stressing its critical role in establishing trust, cultivating authentic connections, and amplifying impact.

Establishing Trust Through Transparency

Ethical marketing concepts emphasize the significance of authenticity, trust and fairness of the operations of the social enterprises. These are the cornerstone for social enterprises in order to present their mission, beliefs, and impacts with confidence and effectively. Genuine representation fosters trust—a valuable product in business where reputation is paramount. Implementing high level transparency goes hand in hand with authenticity, pushing social entrepreneurs to publicly discuss their accomplishments and failures. This transparency encourages stronger bonds and loyalty among stakeholders, reaffirming the organization's dedication to honesty and responsibility. Clear and accessible impact reporting builds confidence by providing stakeholders with insights into the real results of their contributions. Social enterprises that prioritize authenticity, transparency, and impactful reporting not only build their connections with stakeholders, but also fulfil their ethical commitments while driving real social change.

Nurturing Meaningful Stakeholder Relationships

Ethical marketing practices emphasize customer-centric engagement, aiming to build trust and cultivate long term relationships grounded in shared values and respect. Engaging customers in meaningful interactions not only fosters brand loyalty but also encourages advocacy, as satisfied customers become ambassadors of the organization's mission. Similarly, ethical marketing attracts impact investors who are aligned with the enterprise's values and commitment to social impact. By transparently showcasing ethical practices and outcomes, social enterprises can attract investors who prioritize both financial returns and positive societal outcomes. Furthermore, ethical marketing promotes collaboration with like-minded partners who share similar values and goals. By aligning marketing efforts with these partners, social enterprises can leverage collective strengths and amplify their impact, fostering mutually beneficial relationships that drive sustainable growth and societal change. By integrating customer-centric engagement, investor alignment, and partner collaboration, ethical marketing becomes a powerful tool for advancing social enterprises' missions while upholding integrity and accountability.

Elevating Social Impact Through Storytelling

Ethical marketing methods use narrative as a powerful tool for increasing impact and engagement. Social enterprises can motivate action and strengthen stakeholder connections to their goal by creating stories that engage emotionally and highlight practical outcomes. Advocacy and awareness-building are essential components of ethical marketing, allowing companies to educate audiences on urgent social and environmental concerns. This educational strategy not only promotes awareness, but also drives positive societal change via informed decision-making and collaborative actions. Furthermore, ethical marketing strengthens underprivileged communities by highlighting their voices and viewpoints. Giving these groups a forum to tell their stories encourages more empathy, understanding, and solidarity among stakeholders, leading to more inclusive and fair outcomes. By leveraging narrative, advocacy, and empowerment, ethical marketing amplifies the impact of the organisation.

Upholding Responsible Practices

Ethical marketing necessitates responsible sourcing, environmental stewardship, and fair trade practices across the supply chain. Social enterprises promote ethical sourcing by ensuring that goods and resources are ethically procured, with an emphasis on ecologically and socially sustainable processes throughout the value chain. Another important aspect is environmental stewardship, in which businesses promote sustainability and reduce their environmental impact through efficient resource usage and waste reduction techniques. Ethical marketing also promotes fair trade and labour standards, which provide fair wages and safe working conditions for the workers in the supply chain.

Insights

Ethical marketing is more than simply a strategy for social enterprises that reflects their beliefs, dedication to impact, and concern for stakeholders. By employing ethical marketing techniques, social enterprises can foster trust, inspire loyalty, and, eventually, fostering positive transformations.

Guidelines for ethical marketing practices

- **Transparency and Authenticity**

Ethical marketing is based on concepts such as genuine representation, complete transparency, and avoiding greenwashing techniques. It is necessary that all marketing materials appropriately represent the organization's mission, impact, and activities, guaranteeing transparency and authenticity in all communications. Full disclosure means giving clear and open information about funding sources, collaborations, and governance structures, which fosters stakeholder confidence and accountability. Importantly, ethical marketing prevents greenwashing, or making false or exaggerated claims about environmental or social impacts, which may erode trust and jeopardize an organization's integrity. By adhering to these principles, social enterprises sustain ethical standards, foster trust with their audiences, and demonstrate a real commitment to responsible business practices that correspond with their mission.

- **Respect for Stakeholders**

Ethical marketing concepts emphasize the necessity of protecting stakeholders' privacy, adhering to data protection standards, and remaining culturally sensitive. Prioritizing privacy and data protection entails securing personal data and complying with applicable regulations in order to foster trust and protect stakeholders' rights. Cultural sensitivity is essential in developing marketing communications that connect positively across varied cultural contexts, while avoiding stereotypes or objectionable information that may alienate or misrepresent groups. Additionally, ethical marketing stresses responsible stakeholder involvement, inclusive discourse, and actively seeking opinion and criticism. Integrating these principles into marketing tactics demonstrates social enterprise's commitment to ethical practices, boosts credibility, and fosters meaningful connections with stakeholders based on mutual respect and trust.

- **Social and Environmental Responsibility**

Ethical marketing in social enterprises focuses on promoting sustainable practices, fair trade, and community participation as key components of their organisational culture. Advocating for sustainable practices entails advocating products and services that are manufactured and supplied in ways that reduce environmental impact while prioritizing conservation of resources. Implementation of fair trade standards guarantees that all supply chain workers are paid fairly and work in safe, dignified circumstances, demonstrating a commitment to social equality and justice. Another important feature is community involvement, in which social entrepreneurs connect with local communities in a respectful manner while taking into account their specific needs and objectives. By integrating these ethical principles into their marketing strategies, social enterprises not only differentiate themselves in the marketplace but also contribute positively to environmental stewardship, social welfare, and community empowerment, thereby fostering sustainable and inclusive development.

- **Accountability and Impact Measurement**

In social enterprises, ethical marketing practices place an emphasis on responsibility, openness, and continual improvement. Impact reporting is critical, since it requires stakeholders to receive regular and transparent updates on the organization's social and environmental impacts. This builds trust and demonstrates the practical benefits of their assistance. Seeking stakeholder input is also vital for evaluating the efficacy of marketing initiatives and ensuring alignment with their expectations and demands. Social enterprises that actively listen to stakeholders can improve their strategy and efforts, increasing their relevance and impact. Continuous improvement is required, which includes constant review and adaption of marketing techniques based on feedback and thorough impact review. This strategy not only develops connections with stakeholders, but also promotes significant progress towards attaining sustainable development goals and generating positive social change through ethical marketing strategies.

- **Compliance and Legal Standards**

Ethical marketing strategies are critical to social businesses' integrity and sustainability, since they promote trust, credibility, and long-term partnerships with stakeholders. Social organisations that prioritize regulatory compliance adhere to legal norms governing marketing, advertising, and data protection, providing transparency and respecting stakeholders' rights. Adherence to ethical standards established by industry groups and regulatory agencies strengthens the organization's commitment to justice, honesty, and responsible business practices. Fair competition improves credibility by avoiding unethical practices that might hurt competitors or mislead customers.

To summarize, by adhering to these principles and best practices, social enterprises not only match their marketing tactics with their fundamental beliefs, but also demonstrate their commitment to achieving beneficial social and environmental impacts. This commitment not only enhances reputation but also contributes to sustainable growth and meaningful change within communities they serve.

Chapter - 11
Future Trends in Social Enterprise Marketing

Introduction

Marketing for social enterprise is fast evolving, because of evolving customer choices, technological advancements, and an increasing emphasis on sustainability and social impact. This chapter investigates new trends in marketing for social enterprises and provides insights into how these trends might be used to increase impact and reach.

Digital Transformation

Social enterprises are adopting digital technologies to increase their impact and participation through a variety of online platforms. Establishing a strong online presence, including websites, social media platforms, and online marketplaces, has become critical for reaching a larger audience and communicating with stakeholders across the world. The introduction of e-commerce platforms has further strengthened small businesses by allowing direct sales of their products and services, increasing revenue, and increasing market reach beyond conventional borders. Leveraging digital storytelling on multimedia-based platforms like films, infographics, and blogs enables social enterprises to effectively convey their mission, values, and impact stories to a larger global audience. By properly leveraging various digital platforms, social enterprises can increase awareness, increase community participation, and advance their goals of achieving social and environmental change on an impactful scale.

Personalization and Customer Engagement

Technological advancements, notably in data analytics, customer relationship management (CRM), and co-creation, are transforming how social enterprises function and connect with stakeholders. Data analytics technologies give essential insights into customer behavior and preferences, allowing businesses to adjust their marketing strategies and services more precisely and relevantly. CRM systems play an important role in maintaining and developing engagements with customers and stakeholders, increasing engagement and creating long-term loyalty through personalised interactions and targeted communication. Furthermore, the concept of co-creation has gained traction as social entrepreneurs include clients in the development and refining of their goods and services. This collaborative approach not only improves product relevance and satisfaction, but it also fosters a feeling of ownership and togetherness among stakeholders, sustaining the enterprise's mission-driven culture. By leveraging these technological innovations strategically, social enterprises can strengthen connections, drive innovation, and maximize their impact.

Impact Measurement and Reporting

In today's landscape, social enterprises are increasingly integrating strategic approaches to enhance their visibility, credibility, and engagement through impactful practices. They prioritize measuring and reporting their social and environmental impact using standardized metrics like the UN Sustainable Development Goals (SDGs), aiming for clarity and accountability in demonstrating their contributions to global sustainability efforts. Transparency in impact reporting has emerged as a pivotal strategy, distinguishing these enterprises by fostering trust and confidence among consumers and investors. Additionally, leveraging storytelling as a powerful tool, social enterprises craft narratives that vibrantly portray their impact, resonating emotionally with stakeholders and reinforcing their mission-driven initiatives. By embracing these practices—metrics-driven impact measurement, transparent reporting, and compelling storytelling—social enterprises not only strengthen their market positioning but also amplify their transformation efforts.

Collaborative Marketing and Partnerships

Collaboration and partnership activities are critical strategy for social entrepreneurs seeking to increase their impact and influence across the sectors. By forming cross-sector partnerships with corporations, governments, and non-governmental organizations (NGOs), these organizations may utilize complementary capabilities and resources to achieve larger social and environmental goals. Cause marketing collaborations with business partners are becoming more common, allowing both sides to integrate their marketing efforts with social concerns, boosting brand reputation and achieving significant social change. Furthermore, co-marketing activities with like-minded groups enable social entrepreneurs to combine their skills and networks, resulting in campaigns that successfully amplify their ideas and reach larger audiences. These collaborative techniques not only broaden reach and impact, but also encourage creativity, sustainability, and collective action to solve serious sustainability concerns.

Impact Investing and Conscious Consumerism

Impact investment, conscientious consumerism, and great stories are combining to shape the environment for social companies. Impact investing has developed as a major option, garnering funds from investors who value both financial returns and demonstrable social benefit. This infusion of capital not only promotes the growth and viability of social entrepreneurs, but also confirms their role in creating good change. Concurrently, consumer tastes are evolving toward products and services that represent ethical and sustainable practices, driving demand for offerings that match with social responsibility and environmental stewardship principles. Social enterprises capitalize on this trend by using storytelling approaches to clearly explain their impacts and goal, therefore engaging with stakeholders on a deeper, emotional level.

Insights

Marketing for social enterprises are developing in response to shifting customer expectations, technology improvements, and an increased emphasis on ecological sustainability and social impacts. By embracing evolving marketing trends, social enterprises can increase their awareness, engage stakeholders, and optimize their transformative effects.

Technologies shaping the future of social impact marketing

Introduction

Technological advancements are revolutionizing the way social enterprises approach marketing, enabling them to reach new audiences, engage stakeholders, and amplify their impact. This session explores key technologies shaping the future of social impact marketing for social enterprises and how they can be leveraged to drive positive change.

Artificial Intelligence (AI) and Machine Learning

AI-powered solutions are transforming social enterprises marketing methods by enabling personalized marketing, predictive analytics, and interactive consumer interaction. AI algorithms enable social enterprises to examine massive quantities of data to build tailored marketing campaigns that resonate with individual interests and behaviors, establishing stronger connections with their audience. Predictive analytics improves on these efforts by anticipating trends and consumer behaviors, allowing businesses to anticipate demands and fine-tune their strategy proactively. Furthermore, AI-powered chatbots and virtual assistants play an important role in improving user experience by offering real-time customer service and engaging stakeholders in meaningful conversations. These innovations not only maximize operational efficiency, but also help social enterprises to execute more targeted, responsive, cost effective and powerful marketing campaigns, eventually generating increased engagement and establishing long term partnerships.

Augmented Reality (AR) and Virtual Reality (VR)

AR (Augmented Reality) and VR (Virtual Reality) technology are altering the way social enterprises engage stakeholders by providing fascinating experiences, virtual tours, and storytelling. These technologies enable businesses to build interactive and immersive experiences in which stakeholders can engage directly with the organization's goal and impact. Virtual tours employing AR and VR give stakeholders personal information about projects and initiatives, providing an engaging visual experience that improves knowledge and participation. Furthermore, AR and VR are great storytelling tools, allowing social enterprises to express their message in an engaging and immersive manner that connects emotionally with audiences. By leveraging these technologies, social enterprises can increase stakeholder participation, better explain their impact, and develop a greater connection to their mission.

Blockchain Technology

Blockchain technology is transforming the way social organizations approach transparency, efficiency, and accountability throughout their operations. One important use is transparency and traceability, in which blockchain allows firms to give verifiable data about their impact, supply chain operations, and financial transactions. This increases openness by enabling stakeholders to obtain trustworthy data and trace the movement of products and payments in real time. Another blockchain-powered innovation is smart contracts, which automate agreements and transactions like contributions and partnerships, minimizing administrative overhead and guaranteeing that promises are carried out transparently and effectively. Beyond operational efficiency, blockchain improves trust and accountability by storing incontrovertible records that show adherence to ethical standards and promises. Using blockchain technology, social enterprises can enhance connections with stakeholders and improve their reputation and authenticity.

Social Media Marketing

To improve their impact and engagement methods, social entrepreneurs are implementing novel strategies such as social listening, influencer alliances, and user-generated content. Social listening technologies, backed by social media analytics, allow businesses to monitor discussions and trends, collecting important data that guide targeted messaging and responsive engagement strategies. Collaborating with influencers that share the organization's ideals enables social entrepreneurs to magnify their message and reach new, varied audiences who values the influencer's endorsements. Furthermore, promoting user-generated content invites stakeholders to actively participate in sharing their experiences and viewpoints on the organization's objective, which improves authenticity and increases community involvement. These integrated techniques not only build connections with stakeholders, but they also increase the organization's visibility and effectiveness in advancing social and environmental goals.

Data Analytics Technologies

To successfully improve their strategy, social enterprises can rely on data analytics technologies to measure impact, analyse performance, and acquire audience feedbacks. Impact assessment technologies powered by data analytics help businesses to quantify and visualize their social and environmental successes, allowing for more explicit communication of outcomes to stakeholders. By evaluating marketing campaign data, social enterprises can measure performance indicators such as reach, engagement, and conversion rates, allowing them to fine-tune tactics for optimum effect and efficiency. Furthermore, data analytics give useful audience insights by revealing demographics, preferences, and habits. This insight helps businesses to precisely adapt their marketing efforts, ensuring that messages resonate with their intended consumers.

Insights

AI, Augmented reality, Virtual reality, Blockchain, and social media technologies are revolutionizing the way social enterprises approach marketing, allowing them to build more customized, cost effective, engaging, and effective campaigns. By embracing these technologies, social enterprises can increase their coverage, engage stakeholders, and generate positive social change throughout the world.

Opportunities and difficulties in the changing world.

The changing environment of social impact marketing offers both possibilities and difficulties to social enterprises. This session looks at significant trends, opportunities, and problems in the industry, providing insights into how social entrepreneurs should navigate this changing environment to maximize their effect.

- **Opportunities**

Digital marketing and technical improvements are critical in increasing the reach, impact, and effectiveness of social enterprises. For starters, social enterprises can attain global reach by leveraging digital marketing channels and social media platforms to engage with varied audiences all over the world. These platforms not only allow for global distribution of their vision and objectives, but also real-time engagement and contact with stakeholders. Furthermore, storytelling emerges as a powerful tool for social companies, allowing them to communicate their goal and impact via captivating narratives that stimulate emotions and drive action. Collaborations with other organizations, corporations, and individuals increase their reach and influence, building relationships that provide shared value and widen their impact on social concerns.

Furthermore, embracing technological breakthroughs such as AI, blockchain, and VR enables social enterprises to reinvent their engagement methods, increase transparency, and generate significant social change via interactive and immersive experiences. Using these tools and methods, social enterprises can successfully communicate their vision, engage stakeholders, and accelerate beneficial social reforms on a global scale.

- **Challenges**

Social enterprises encounter a number of problems in their marketing campaigns, which can have an influence on their efficacy and reach. The digital gap, which separates people with and those without access to technology, is a significant barrier that limits the reach of digital marketing methods to different audiences. To build trust and credibility in a competitive environment, social enterprises must prioritize transparency, authenticity, and responsibility in their marketing activities, as well as ensure that their messaging is consistent with their mission and values. Resource restrictions, such as restricted finance, personnel shortages, and skill gaps, make it even more difficult for social entrepreneurs to develop effective marketing strategies that may double their impact.

Furthermore, these enterprises must navigate a complicated and growing legal environment, particularly in terms of data protection and marketing activities across many jurisdictions. To effectively involve stakeholders and create long-term social change, these issues must be addressed by strategic planning, creative techniques, and a commitment to ethical practices.

Strategies for Success

Social enterprises should focus on several important methods to increase marketing effectiveness and impact. To begin, they must clearly express their vision, values, and impacts in order to develop trust and confidence among stakeholders. This transparency not only strengthens their image, but also draws support from individuals and organizations who share their ideals. Using data analytics and audience insights, social enterprises can adjust their marketing messages and campaigns to connect with their target audiences' needs and habits, therefore increasing engagement and effectiveness. Collaboration with like-minded organizations, businesses, and individuals broadens their reach and influence, resulting in synergies that grow their audience and generate collective impacts.

Embracing innovation and incorporating new technology into marketing tactics is critical for remaining competitive and generating significant change in the continually changing world of social entrepreneurship. Integrating these tactics allows social businesses to successfully convey their vision, engage stakeholders authentically, and generate positive social impact on a larger scale.

Insight

The evolving landscape of social impact marketing presents both opportunities and challenges for social enterprises. By leveraging the power of storytelling, collaboration, and technology, social enterprises can maximize their impact and drive positive social change in the world.

Chapter - 12
Caste Study
Vetiver based Women Micro-entrepreneurship: Building Resilience through Mutually Benefited Interaction between Nature and Local Community

Introduction

Idukki district in Kerala, India, lies in the Western Ghats, faces escalating environmental challenges exacerbated by climate change. In this biodiversity hotspot, women play a vital role in agriculture, yet they encounter significant socio-economic barriers. Responding to these challenges, the Peermade Development Society (PDS), an NGO operating with a mission of empowering the rural communities in the region, has launched the Vetiver based Women Micro-entrepreneurship initiative. By reviving Vetiver grass for soil conservation and empowering women through craft-based micro-enterprises, PDS is fostering economic resilience and ecological sustainability. This article explores how this initiative integrates conservation with economic empowerment, showcasing its transformative impact on both local livelihoods and environmental sustainability.

Need for intervention: A Biodiversity Hotspot under Threat

Idukki district in Kerala, India, is part of the Western Ghats, one of the world's major biodiversity hotspots. This region, characterized by its sloping terrain, faces increasing challenges due to unpredictable weather patterns. Intense rainfall, storms, droughts, and disruptions in monsoon patterns lead to flash floods, soil erosion, landslides, and significant crop losses. With 45% of its 4,358 sq. km area covered by forests, Idukki's land use reflects its high-altitude environment. About 81% of land holdings are less than one hectare, primarily employing mixed cropping systems. The district is known for cash crops like pepper, cardamom, coffee, tea, coconut, and rubber. The dependency of spice crops on stable climatic conditions means that climate change has had an accelerated and adverse impact on the agro-ecological system of the region. Additionally, soil erosion has resulted in the runoff of topsoil, leading to decreased fertility and further jeopardizing agricultural productivity.

Although, in the region even, women play a vital yet underappreciated role in agriculture, engaging in crop cultivation, livestock management, and organic farming. Despite their significant contributions, they face challenges such as limited land ownership, restricted access to resources and modern technology, heavy workloads, health risks, and socio-economic barriers stemming from patriarchal norms.

The Foundation of Agriculture: Soil Health

Soil health is critical for sustainable agriculture. It enhances the resilience of farms and supply chains to the effects of increased climate variability. Healthy soils act as carbon sinks, reducing greenhouse gas emissions and increasing carbon sequestration, thereby playing a key role in mitigating climate change. Effective soil management practices such as soil restoration, multi-cropping systems, no-till farming, cover cropping, nutrient management, manuring, improved grazing, water conservation and harvesting, efficient irrigation, and agroforestry help improve soil organic carbon content and reduce carbon loss from the soil.

The Interventions of Peermade Development Society (PDS)

Since its inception in 1980, the Peermade Development Society (PDS), a non-governmental organization based in Peermade, Idukki, has been committed to intervening in local agro-ecosystems to promote sustainable farming practices. PDS engages in rural empowerment activities, organic farming promotion, biodiversity conservation, research and development, and the processing and marketing of organic products. Their mission is to empower small and marginal farmers and create a resilient agricultural value chain in the rural areas of the Western Ghats. PDS has a well-established farm extension system, along with facilities for organic Spices processing and quality assurance.

The Strategy: Reviving Traditional Wisdom- Vetiver Grass

In the past, farmers in Idukki used Vetiver (Chrysopogon zizanioides) for soil conservation and Ayurvedic medicine. However, over time, this traditional bio-engineering system fell out of favour. Recognizing the ecological benefits of Vetiver, PDS revived the practice of planting

Vetiver grass, which is native to the Western Ghats, to combat soil erosion and nutrient loss in the hilly terrain of Idukki. PDS developed Vetiver slips in their nursery to supply to spice farmers for planting along contours. Vetiver grass, with its deep and fibrous root system, binds the soil, prevents landslides, slows water runoff, traps sediment, filters out nutrients, and retains soil moisture. When planted in rows, Vetiver forms a living porous barrier that reduces the erosive power of water, allowing more time for infiltration and trapping eroded material. This effective hedge reduces soil erosion, conserves soil moisture, and enhances soil organic carbon pools, a key objective of regenerative agriculture.

Vetiver roots, known for their aromatic properties and used in Ayurvedic medicine for their antiseptic, detoxifying, and cooling effects, are bought back by PDS for traditional medicinal formulations. Recognizing the underutilized potential of Vetiver leaves, which grow profusely, PDS conceived an initiative to create sustainable packaging materials for organic spices using these leaves.

The Action: Empowering Women through Micro-entrepreneurship

In partnership with some agencies PDS trained a group of homemakers to craft gift boxes from Vetiver leaves, forming a self-help group (SHG). These women received support in research and development to identify the best Vetiver varieties for crafting, develop new product ideas, and connect their crafts to potential markets. Training sessions on governance, financial management, and debt management were also provided to ensure the group's sustainability and success.

Purpose, Passion and Profit: Impactful marketing Strategies for Social Enterprises

Currently, the women's group collects Vetiver grass from various farms, processes it, and crafts baskets. PDS purchases these baskets and markets it as organic spice gift boxes. This initiative offers compelling value propositions rooted in sustainability, empowerment of women, cultural heritage preservation, and innovative product development. It stands out for its eco-friendly practices, empowering local women through entrepreneurship, revitalizing traditional knowledge, and introducing innovative uses of natural resources. These elements combine to create a unique offering that not only promotes environmental stewardship but also fosters social inclusivity and celebrates local cultural practices.

This initiative not only provides an additional source of income for the women but also promotes the sustainable use of Vetiver, reinforcing the ecological benefits of planting this grass.

An Analysis of the marketing mix

The marketing mix, often referred to as the 4 Ps (Product, Price, Place, Promotion), for the Vetiver-based Women Micro-entrepreneurship initiative can be detailed as follows:

- **Product**

Vetiver Baskets and Gift Boxes: Crafted from Vetiver leaves by the women's self-help group, these baskets are used as packaging for organic spices. This eco-friendly packages adds the value of organic spices by highlighting the aspects of sustainability and eco-friendliness

Product Features

> ➢ Eco-friendly: Made from sustainable materials.
> ➢ Cultural Heritage: Revives traditional practices of using Vetiver.

- **Price**

Pricing Strategy:
> ➢ Premium Pricing: Reflects the high quality, eco-friendly nature, and artisanal craftsmanship of the products.
> ➢ Value-based Pricing: Based on the unique value propositions of sustainability, women empowerment, and cultural heritage.

Cost Considerations:
> ➢ Production Costs: Costs of collecting and processing Vetiver, crafting the baskets, and packaging spices.
> ➢ Training and Development: Investment in skill development and capacity building for the women involved.

- **Place**

Distribution Channels:
> ➢ Direct Sales: Through Peermade Development Society's network, local markets, and events.
> ➢ Retail Partnerships: In Collaboration with gift shops, tourism industry outlets, and corporate gifting services.

> Online Sales: E-commerce platforms like PDS's own e-commerce website, other e-com sites and social media channels for wider reach.

Geographical Reach:
> Local Market: Primarily within the Idukki district and nearby regions.

> National and International Markets: Targeting eco-conscious consumers and niche markets globally.

- **Promotion**
  > Storytelling: Emphasizing the stories of women empowerment, ecological conservation, and traditional knowledge.

  > Social Media Campaigns: Leveraging platforms like Instagram, Facebook, and Twitter to showcase the products and the impact of the initiative.

  > Partnerships: Collaborating with environmental women's organizations, international development agencies, and other like-minded NGOs to spread awareness.

  > Events and Exhibitions: Participating in fairs, expos, and conferences related to sustainable agriculture, women entrepreneurship, and organic products.

  > Awards and Recognitions: Highlighting international awards and recognitions to build credibility and attract attention.

Analysis of the existing and potential marketing strategies

This is a comprehensive analysis of the marketing strategies currently adopted and those that can be adopted to promote their product—the handcrafted Vetiver gift box by the Vetiver-based Women Micro-entrepreneurship initiative.

- **Storytelling and Narrative Marketing**
  - Impactful Stories: Highlighting personal stories of the women involved, showcasing how their lives have changed through the initiative.
  - Environmental Impact: Emphasizing the ecological benefits of planting Vetiver and its role in soil conservation, climate change adaptation and enhancement of local agro eco-system.
  - Cultural Heritage: Promoting the traditional use of Vetiver in the region and its significance in local culture.

- **Eco-friendly and Sustainable Branding**
  - Green Messaging: Emphasizing the eco-friendly nature of the products, aligning with the increasing consumer demand for sustainable products.
  - Certifications and Labels: Obtaining certifications related to organic and sustainable practices from government agencies and other national and international agencies to build trust and authenticity.

- **Community Engagement and Social Responsibility**
  - Local Partnerships: Collaborating with local businesses, NGOs, and community organizations to promote the initiative.
  - Corporate Social Responsibility (CSR): Partnering with companies and corporations looking to enhance their CSR profiles through sustainable and socially responsible projects.

- **Digital Marketing**
  - Social Media Campaigns: Using platforms like Instagram, Facebook, and Twitter and PDS's own c-commerce platforms to reach a wider audience, share updates, and engage with followers.

- Content Marketing: Creating and sharing content such as blogs, videos, and infographics about the benefits of Vetiver, the women's stories, and the ecological impact.
- E-commerce Presence: Selling products through online marketplaces and own website to reach a global audience.

- **Participation in Events and Exhibitions**
  - Trade Fairs and Expos: Participating in organic product fairs and sustainability expos such as organic and millets expo, Biofach etc, and women entrepreneurship events to showcase products and network with potential buyers.
  - Conferences and Seminars: Presenting the initiative at relevant national and international conferences to gain visibility and attract partners and supporters.

- **Product Diversification and Innovation**
  - Innovative Products: Developing new products using Vetiver, such as eco-friendly packaging, home décor items, and wellness products, to cater to different market segments.
  - Customization: Offering customized gift boxes for corporate gifting and special occasions to attract more customers.

- **Market Research and Consumer Feedback**
  - Understanding Market Needs: Conducting market research to understand consumer preferences and trends in eco-friendly and artisanal products.
  - Feedback Mechanism: Implementing a system to gather and analyse consumer feedback for continuous improvement of products and services.

- **Strategic Pricing**
  - Value-based Pricing: Setting prices based on the perceived value of the products, considering the craftsmanship, sustainability, and social and environmental impact.
  - Promotional Offers: Providing discounts and special offers during festive seasons and special events to boost sales.

- **Public Relations and Media Coverage**
  - ➤ Press Releases: Issuing press releases to local and national media about major milestones, awards, and events.
  - ➤ Media Coverage: Securing coverage in newspapers, magazines, and online publications to increase visibility and credibility.

- **Collaboration and Networking**
  - ➤ Strategic Partnerships: Building alliances with organizations and businesses that share similar values of sustainability and social responsibility.
  - ➤ Networking: Engaging with influencers, thought leaders, and industry experts to promote the initiative and gain endorsements.
  - ➤ Volunteering: In collaboration with schools, universities and like-minded development institutes, the group can deploy volunteers and trainees for market research, product development, story creation, online promotion and raising awareness.

By effectively implementing these marketing strategies, the Vetiver-based Women Micro-entrepreneurship initiative can effectively promote its products, enhance its brand image, and achieve its goals of social and environmental impact.

Multi-dimensional Impact

The Vetiver Women Micro-entrepreneurship initiative by PDS has catalysed the long term sustainability of the socio-agrological fabric of the region by transforming ecological activities into economic opportunities. By reviving the traditional practice of planting Vetiver for soil conservation and integrating it into the value chain as a women empowerment initiative, PDS ensures the sustainability of conservation efforts. This initiative highlights the mutually beneficial interaction between nature and local communities, showcasing how environmental conservation can drive social and economic empowerment. The additional family income generated through women's entrepreneurship ensures that conservation activities are economically viable, promoting resilience and regeneration of the agro-ecosystem in the Western Ghats region.

- Economic Empowerment: Around 100 women have gained financial independence, earning a sustainable income through Vetiver basket making.
- Skill Development: Women have acquired valuable skills in crafting and financial management, enhancing their entrepreneurial capabilities.
- Market Recognition: The initiative has received international recognition through the International Micro-Entrepreneurship Award in Paris in 2014.
- Social Empowerment: By integrating women into the spice value chain, the project has reduced their financial dependency and enhanced their social standing within the community.
- Ecological Conservation: Farmers are encouraged to plant Vetiver across their farms to prevent soil erosion, hold rain water in the soil and enhance other ecosystem services.

Insights

This Vetiver micro-entrepreneurship project exemplifies how integrating women into the spice value chain reduces financial dependency and promotes ecological regeneration. This initiative highlights the synergistic relationship between nature and local communities, driving sustainable development in the Western Ghats region.

Appendix
Resources for Social Enterprise Marketing

Marketing a social enterprise involves a combination of strategic thought, creativity, and the effective tools. This session gives a detailed reference to the tools, templates, and resources that may assist social businesses improve their marketing efforts and accomplish both economic and social impact objectives. Please note that this list is indicative and not exhaustive. The writer has no affiliations or interests in any of the sources or companies mentioned. It is advised to conduct your own research and analysis before utilizing any of the services listed.

Market Research Tools

Effective market research is the foundation of any successful marketing strategy. For social enterprises, understanding the needs, preferences, and behaviors of their target audience is crucial. Here are some tools that can help:

- SurveyMonkey: An easy-to-use platform for creating and distributing surveys. It offers a variety of question types and analysis tools to gather detailed insights.
- Google Forms: A free tool that allows you to create surveys and collect responses quickly. It's integrated with Google Sheets for data analysis.
- Typeform: Known for its interactive and engaging survey design, Typeform can help increase response rates and gather qualitative data.
- Qualtrics: An advanced survey platform suitable for in-depth market research and data analysis, offering powerful features for customization and reporting.

Customer Relationship Management (CRM) Tools

Managing relationships with customers and stakeholders is vital for social enterprises. CRM tools help streamline communication, track interactions, and manage data effectively.

- Salesforce: A comprehensive CRM platform that helps manage customer relationships, track interactions, and analyze data.
- HubSpot CRM: A free CRM tool that offers contact management, email tracking, and sales automation. It's suitable for small to medium-sized social enterprises.
- Zoho CRM: Affordable CRM software with a variety of features, including customization options, making it ideal for growing businesses.
- Insightly: Combines CRM and project management capabilities, helping social enterprises manage relationships and projects efficiently.

Social Media Management Tools

Social media is a powerful channel for reaching and engaging with your audience. These tools can help manage your social media presence effectively:

- Hootsuite: Allows you to manage and schedule posts across multiple social media platforms, monitor conversations, and analyze performance.

- Buffer: A user-friendly tool for scheduling social media posts and analyzing their performance. It's known for its simplicity and efficiency.

- Sprout Social: Offers comprehensive social media management features, including scheduling, monitoring, and analytics.

- Later: Focused on Instagram, later helps plan and schedule visual content, providing a clear overview of your social media calendar.

Content Creation Tools

Creating compelling content is essential for engaging your audience and communicating your social impact. These tools can help:

- Canva: A design tool that allows you to create social media graphics, presentations, and other marketing materials easily, even without design experience.

- Adobe Spark: Enables the creation of stunning graphics, web pages, and video stories, perfect for storytelling and visual content.

- Piktochart: An infographic maker that helps turn complex data into engaging visuals, useful for impact reporting and presentations.

- Lumen5: Converts blog posts into engaging videos, making it easier to repurpose content for social media.

Email Marketing Tools

Email marketing remains a powerful tool for communication and engagement. Here are some tools that can enhance your email campaigns:

- Mailchimp: An email marketing platform offering automation, customizable templates, and detailed analytics.

- Constant Contact: Provides email marketing services with customizable templates, list segmentation, and analytics.

- Sendin Blue: Offers email marketing, SMS marketing, and automation features, suitable for comprehensive marketing campaigns.

- Active Campaign: Combines email marketing, automation, and CRM capabilities, providing a holistic approach to customer engagement.

Analysis Tools

Measuring the effectiveness of your marketing efforts is crucial for continuous improvement. These tools can help track and analyze data:

- Google Analytics: A free tool for tracking and analyzing website traffic and user behavior.
- Hotjar: Provides heatmaps, session recordings, and feedback tools to understand user interactions and improve user experience.
- Mixpanel: Offers advanced analytics for tracking user interactions with web and mobile applications.
- Kissmetrics: Behavioral analytics and engagement tools that help optimize marketing strategies and improve user experience.

Templates for Social Enterprise Marketing

Templates can save time and ensure consistency in your marketing efforts. Here are some useful templates:

Persona Templates

Creating detailed personas is essential for understanding your audience. These templates can help:

- Xtensio Persona Template: A detailed template for creating buyer personas, including demographics, behaviors, goals, and pain points.
- HubSpot Persona Template: A free, customizable template to define your target audience, helping you tailor your marketing efforts.
- Buffer Persona Template: A simple, user-friendly template to map out your ideal customer profiles and understand their needs.

Marketing Plan Templates

A well-structured marketing plan guides your efforts and ensures alignment with your goals. Here are some templates to consider:

- HubSpot Marketing Plan Template: A comprehensive template that covers all aspects of your marketing strategy, from goals to tactics and metrics.

- Smartsheet Marketing Plan Template: A detailed template for organizing marketing activities, timelines, and budgets.
- Venngage Marketing Plan Template: Visual templates for creating engaging and professional marketing plans, ideal for presentations and internal use.

Content Calendar Templates

Planning your content in advance helps maintain consistency and manage your resources effectively. These templates can help:

- CoSchedule Content Calendar Template: Plan and schedule your content marketing efforts across various channels.
- Trello Content Calendar Template: Use Trello boards to organize and track your content pipeline, with customizable boards and cards.
- Google Sheets Content Calendar Template: A simple, shareable template for planning content, suitable for collaborative teams.

Campaign Planning Templates

Effective campaign planning ensures your efforts are coordinated and aligned with your goals. Here are some useful templates:

- HubSpot Campaign Planning Kit: Templates and resources for planning and executing marketing campaigns, including timelines and budget tracking.
- Airtable Marketing Campaign Template: Use Airtable to organize and track your marketing campaigns, with customizable views and fields.
- Miro Campaign Planning Template: Visual collaboration templates for brainstorming and planning marketing campaigns, suitable for team use.

In addition to tools and templates, various venues can provide valuable insights and learning opportunities:

- Connect with peers and learn from their experiences through these networking and community platforms.
- LinkedIn Groups: Join groups related to social entrepreneurship and marketing to connect with like-minded professionals and share insights.

- Social Enterprise World Forum: An annual event and online community for social enterprises worldwide, offering networking and learning opportunities.

- B Corps Community: Connect with certified B Corporations committed to social and environmental performance, and learn from their marketing practices.

- Meetup: Find local groups and events focused on social entrepreneurship and marketing, providing opportunities for networking and collaboration.

Conclusion

Marketing for social enterprises requires a systematic strategy supported by the appropriate tools, templates, and resources. By exploring these tools, social enterprises can improve their marketing efforts, gain a better understanding of their consumers, and increase their social impact. Whether you are just getting started or want to improve your existing tactics, the tools, templates, and resources presented in this chapter will give a solid basis for success. Embrace these tools and resources to propel your social enterprise ahead, resulting in substantial change and long-term impact.

References

- https://socialenterprise.us/about/social-enterprise
- http://secouncil.ca/en/
- https://elaw.klri.re.kr/eng_service/lawView.do?hseq=24346&lang=ENG
- https://eur-lex.europa.eu/LexUriServ/LexUriServ.do?uri=COM:2011:0682:FIN:EN:PDF
- https://www.sebi.gov.in/sebi_data/commondocs/AIFregulations2012_p.pdf
- https://www.rbi.org.in/CommonPerson/english/Scripts/Notification.aspx?Id=2613
- Rural health statistics by the Ministry of Health and Family Welfare, Government of India
- Lok Sabha Un starred Question NO. 1899 Answered ON 13.03.2023
- Situation Assessment of Agricultural Households and Land and Livestock Holding, 2019
- https://www.britishcouncil.in/sites/default/files/social_enterprise_policy_landscape_in_india_0.pdf
- https://www.ted.com/talks/simon_sinek_how_great_leaders_inspire_action?language=en&geo=hi
- American Marketing Association, AMA Dictionary.
- Impact Management and Measurement Concepts by investment impact index, SA
- The United Nations Development Programme (UNDP) website
- Stanford social innovation review
- Feor, L.; Clarke, A.; Dougherty, I. Social Impact Measurement: A Systematic Literature Review and Future Research Directions. World 2023, 4, 816-837. https://doi.org/10.3390/world4040051
- https://movingworlds.org/social-entrepreneurship-guide.

www.ingramcontent.com/pod-product-compliance
Lightning Source LLC
LaVergne TN
LVHW061618070526
838199LV00078B/7326